Extramuros

TWENTIETH-CENTURY CONTINENTAL FICTION

EXTRAMUROS

by

Jesús Fernández Santos

Translated from the Spanish by
Helen R. Lane

New York • COLUMBIA UNIVERSITY PRESS • *1984*

Library of Congress Cataloging in Publication Data
Fernández Santos, Jesús.
Extramuros.

(Twentieth-Century Continental fiction)
Translation of: Extramuros.
I. Title. II. Series.
PQ6611.E657E9513 1984 863'.64 83-19018
ISBN 0-231-05552-8

*Columbia University Press gratefully acknowledges
the assistance of
the Comité Conjunto Hispano-
Norteamericano para Asuntos Educativos y Culturales
in the preparation of this translation.*

Columbia University Press
New York   Guildford, Surrey

Clothbound editions of Columbia University Press Books are
Smyth-sewn and printed on permanent and durable acid-free paper

Extramuros

Chapter One

OUTSIDE the walls the moon stood still. Beyond the king's highway it hovered motionless above the city, above its towers and walls, looking down upon the high meadows where each week the temporary market stalls were set up. The massive walls now revealed the ground plan of their flanks, their square pinnacles, their emblazoned gates with their torches of pitch and tow stirred by the solemn breath of the gusts of wind. From afar there came the intermittent sound of the river lending life to the night, the voice of the shimmering plain, the opaque silence of the earth, of the bare hills and the barren furrows.

Everything had congealed, stopped, died beneath the mantle of that cold light, at the foot of frozen clouds like the white spun threads of an invisible distaff, like spectral flocks of sheep, driven, harried, divided by the wind's swift dogs.

The light made the water-mills of the river, ordinarily still and silent, rise from their ashes, from their nightly death, made the rooftops and enclosures gleam, covered the rough roads, the frightening calvaries with tiny crystals, beyond the walls, beyond the sharp-pointed spires of their towers. They

I

could be seen pointing to the mother of all things, to the Lady of the Night, white, burnished, naked, banishing by her presence not only the stars but also the clouds and the birds. It was her icy mantle, her realm of bitter cold, not of warm shadows, her voice a mere thread like the whisper of oars in the river that sighingly wends its way past the town.

Everything, the city, the hills, and the highway skirting them could be made out there in the distance, on the other side of the worn lattice. By day, on the other hand, droves of carriers could be seen with the white harvest of bread loaded on their stout mules, calmly confronting the arduous climb up to the market, flocks of sheep like sleepwalkers, herded along the narrow paths with loud shouts, people on foot, in litters, cavaliers pacing along, slow and stately, sumptuous corteges, indifferent to the cold wind of the sierra, disappearing in the distance, making their way through the dust to court.

All that could be contemplated, felt, glimpsed beyond our walls, to the rhythm of our labors or our prayers, depending on the hour, on what the day had brought, on our devotion, depending on what the Almighty, the source of both hardships and favors, decreed for our benefit.

And so it was that one night, at the hour of matins when the community was in the choir, He decreed that my sister should fall to the ground, or rather, to the oft-mended, broken floor of wooden planks. It may have been that it was the sickness that comes from the change of season or the miserable food of that year full of so many long privations, or her eagerness to be found deserving of those first vows that we so yearned to take, but she lay there insensible on the floor. We hurried to her and did our best to raise her to her feet, and since the prioress decided not to summon the doctor in view of the lateness of the hour, she ordered us to take her out into the fresh air by the door, as though the cold night air and our prayers were capable of driving away the illness and making her better. But such a remedy was not necessary. Little by little she began to raise her head all by herself as the sisters exchanged agitated glances, as alert as though she had come back from another world, from beyond the cloister, from farther off than even the walls of the city, perhaps from those very stars that were again shivering overhead.

Little by little she stood up, putting her foot, her hands forward with the aid of the other sisters, groping her way back to her cell, where there at least awaited her the pitiful protection of the blanket which, although thin and worn, was nonetheless of more help to her than that icy night dampness and the moon hiding from sight overhead.

The entire night went by with her sighing and shivering and beseeching the Lord to give her the strength at least to stand on her feet, as she tried to do several times, struggling to go out to the privy or return to the choir to follow the hymns. But each new attempt ended in defeat, each hope in a new setback. And thus we spent the night together, she watching the new day dawn beyond the tiny little window, I praying, fighting off my drowsiness and that cold, as black as a demon, that made one's arms and legs ache. As the sun appeared over the garden walls, the bell at the main entrance rang, announcing a visitor. In a few moments the door of the cell opened and the prioress, accompanied by our old doctor, entered. His cheeks were still red from the damp night air and his hands like mere tendons about to break through his transparent skin. Bundled up in his cape that didn't even come down over his knees, he looked like a great bald bird that the cruel January wind had driven to seek shelter amid those wretched walls.

The prioress explained to the doctor how the sister had taken ill, and upon taking her pulse, examining the depths of her eyes, consulting the various humors, he solemnly delivered himself of the opinion, after thinking it over for a moment, that what was most serious was the patient's extreme weakness. Her grave exhaustion could, however, be overcome with a diet of wine, bread, and meat in abundance and work that consisted only of brief, light tasks.

He spoke these words and then immediately fell silent; it was as if he had looked around as he spoke and really seen that wretched cell with its broken floor tiles, its bed and its washbasin, and the walls threatening to fall apart at any moment, with the adobe bricks showing through the cracks.

He fell silent, seeing by the light of the oil lamp my sister's blushing cheeks and the look on the mother superior's face as they listened to his voice, knowing how little bread there was because of the drought, how we had last eaten meat on the feast day of our patron saint, and drunk our last wine a little while later, before our cellar went dry for good.

A moment later, there before my sister's bed, before her worn, gaunt face, he must have remembered what hard and miserable times these had been, what lonely years for her soul and her wretched body. Hence he said no more as I pulled the upper fold of the sheet up over my sister's lips, covering her deep, labored breathing, the little white cloud that rose in the air each time her breath quickened.

She was like the birds that the freezing cold of winter fells:

4

so weak and helpless, scarcely able to breathe, still struggling to fly, to stir, to hoist herself up into the branches again.

As I accompanied the doctor and the prioress, the two of them dejected and deep in thought, to the gate, I asked him if she would have any more fainting spells. He answered that she was still very ill and more or less insensible, that if the Lord did not help her, there was very little then that men, with all their knowledge, could do to try to give her back her health and strength.

And thus it was, for many a day and many a long hour, my sister sighing deeply and I maintaining that she would soon be over her illness; she closing her eyes like one who is bidding this world farewell and I taking her hands in mine, trying to relieve her loneliness, struggling to kindle a spark of hope in her.

News of the house soon reached our chaplain's ears. The doctor passed the word on to him almost immediately, and after much thought, the two of them agreed, as was only proper, to inform our superiors of the situation.

A vain effort, since times must have been no better in the town in which they resided. There too the Devil was no doubt sowing his harvest of worldly ills: faith dwindling, charity forgotten, hope waning because of the drought.

Though with regard to faith, Our Lord never forsook us, the rain forgot us winter after winter, summer after summer, leaving not a single blade of grass for many leagues around, not a single running brook, nor a single sprouting furrow.

It was one of those famous calamities that the Holy Book tells of. The water disappeared from rivers and springs, and rain from the clouds. The countryside breathed forth dust, affliction, and misery. According to those who visited our house in search of a bit of bread and broth, it was a sad thing to see the ears of grain just forming and already dead in the sun, neither ripe nor in their proper season, the outlying fields parched and the cattle left to wander, searching as best they could, along footpaths and trails, for what heaven and earth were denying them.

In days gone by the king's highway came to life when the sun set, full of passing mules and horses, corteges and carts. As seen now from behind the lattice, it appeared to lie deserted in the distance, like a foreboding sign of what was soon to come.

And so it came to pass that as our misfortunes grew, as the sky remained cloudless, the land dry, and the paths empty, the second calamity, ever lying in wait, befell us, as though summoned by its sister.

There came a very bad sickness which left people weak, disabled, and even more dejected: the plague, that scourge that every so often decimates our towns and the court, that makes people flee the city, abandoning their worldly goods and their homes and even the most beloved members of their family. It arrived without warning, without prior notice, as if in secret, and though we had been expecting it for some time, the memory of its ravages in times past was enough to sow panic in people, body and soul. Those of my sisters whose faith was strongest were of the opinion that it was an easy thing to pass on to the Beyond and see Our Lord God, but I, being no doubt of less firm faith, more attached to the things of this world, was unable to feel myself a mere passing stranger here below, nor to turn my mind willingly to heavenly things, nor to appreciate the profit therein as preached to us each day by our confessor, telling us how those who are truly alive live up there in heaven above our heads, whereas those here below lose everything in their blindness, clinging to mere transitory joys.

The prioress recommended that we offer our trials and tribulations to the Lord, Who when all was said and done was simply testing us by such sacrifices, but I was not able to understand how such misfortunes earned us the title of blessed, nor how those poor people who arrived each day before our gate had earned it by their dignity amid suffering, how all this poverty, such black years as these were meant, as she maintained, to enhance our glory in the midst of destitution.

Our traditional poverty, as laid down by the rules of our order, scorning worldly goods, pomp, and abundance, was only fitting and proper, but our privation, not a new thing certainly but crueler and sadder than in previous years, was killing all happiness and hope within us, as though the Lord had forsaken us, mayhap through some grave fault of ours.

In vain the prioress explained to us how those terrible trials were a mark of glory and special recompense for the community; at night on our way to the choir when our feet brushed earth that lay unsettled on graves dug only recently, we asked ourselves which of us would be the first, which of us Our Lord would call to Him before the dawn of another day.

I for my part—I said to myself—have no desire for such blazons or banners for myself. Since I came here to serve the

Lord, it is better that I do so alive than dead, working with my hands or raising my voice in praise in the choir, embroidering or laboring in the garden, rather than lying beneath the earth in that dusty corner of the cloister.

Those were my thoughts, scarcely tranquil ones, as I watched over my sister, whose health was declining with each passing day. I remained at her side every moment that I could steal from choir or kitchen, almost always reading aloud to her from pious books, lives of saints who had earned heaven's peace by their good deeds here below. The book that I was reading from was too much for me at times, the pages little by little seemed as heavy to me as flagstones; along with the torment in my soul I suffered from aching arms and grew so drowsy I could scarcely go on. My thoughts wandered off to all those virgins and valiant men, to the great gifts of grace that the Lord had granted them, to their martyrdom and steadfast devotion, to the way in which their will had prevailed, gaining for themselves and for their communities every manner of good fortune.

I thought of our poor house and immediately tears came to my eyes. At other times, however, anger filled my heart like a flame invading the cell, consuming my sister and me, destroying the whole convent, erasing every last trace of gentle patience, in the sisters, in the community. Then, in the late afternoon above all, as the sun was setting, at that hour when the countryside seems to draw living breath, our chief enemy there inside the walls appeared: that perverse humor, melancholy.

At those moments, I could not help but share my sister's mood, the two of us fallen silent, my reason cast in shadow, darkened, like a stranger to myself, listless, dispirited, the book in my hands.

8

She would then take it in hers and in her weak voice would go on where I had left off, and this time it happened to be the life of a saint famous not only for her many virtues and supernatural gifts, but also for having raised her community from its miserable state to that of a meeting-place and pilgrimage site for all manner of illustrious persons.

The convent renovated and its order having spread far and wide, its fame and affluence grew to such a point that it came to be the mother house and head of many other convents in various regions and districts. It was in the Sierras de Córdoba that Our Savior appeared to the saint, touching her hands, His fingers leaving His own wounds in them forever. Shortly thereafter, the lance-wound of Golgotha appeared in her side, and soon her life changed altogether. She thenceforth ate and drank almost nothing, her one sustenance being Holy Communion, and kept very nearly constant vigil, devoting to prayer the hours that the other sisters spent sleeping.

She had a very personal vision of the Sacrament, seeing it as a child surrounded by angels; she never removed the cilice from her flesh, and her feet were never shod either in leather or esparto, even in the coldest seasons and the most inclement weather. Her virtues and merit were such that, year after year, she was elected abbess of her house, and attained such great renown that the Empress herself sent her portrait to her as a keepsake.

The story of her life, which she had dictated or written down in her own hand, became in those days my sister's best gift, her best medicine, the only balm capable of banishing her afflictions in those long days of convalescence.

At times she would thoughtfully raise her face, gazing beyond the window. At other times, in dreams, she would mutter as though the memories of the day were churning in her mind. No sort of medicine helped, save the book and the saint and the blessings that she had procured for her reborn, well-endowed house.

She often talked to me of all that when we began to go out into the cloister garden, bound for the orchard, when the prioress, with her experience of those who have often dealt with this sickness, bade me help her, with tact and patience, not by ordering her about, something which she would surely resist, but by showing great affection and concern for her. And so, in order to occupy her in some way and leave her no time for self-pity, I began to rouse her from her bed in mid-morning, when the sun was not yet unbearably hot, and on reaching the reservoir, we would tarry there till the happy sound of the bell ringing from the kitchen reached our ears.

Long hours in which the chirping of the sparrows and the monotonous chirring of the cicadas announcing the heat of August made the two of us forget bitter moments. I some-times prayed to God that it be His will to give me her mal-ady, that sickness of my sister and companion, but the Lord did not listen to me, or much better put: she began to re-cover, mayhap because of my prayers. In any event, she com-menced to eat again with a better will, her fever went away, and no more purges or bleeding were necessary. She became so much better that soon she was walking by herself and even logically reasoning our present situation through, though the conclusions we arrived at were very different. She thought— and told me—that it was not right, in view of the disasters that had befallen our house, the precarious state we were in, to leave its fate entirely in the hands of others. If the usual remedy—alms and harvests—were lacking, we, as workers in the community, ought to seek from other sources what the world had once generously given us but now persisted in refusing us.

In vain I answered that it was better to have a small house that was ours than a large one that was not ours, dependent upon other people's money and favors; we were better off free in the community than slaves of the town, of aid begged for and in the end eluding us. But something happened that proved her entirely right and me altogether wrong, an event which I shall recount in a moment and which came to be the cornerstone, the keystone of the arch that my sister was erecting all by herself. I do not know if that was when the ruin of all of us, of our honored name and our fame in the world began, but it is certain truth that it was then that the Devil began to work toward our downfall, as is his habit night and day, without rest or repose.

It so happened that our chaplain's letter, giving an account of the dire hardships that we were enduring, reached the provincial, who decided to visit the house in person. Perhaps he had a little free time after having preached at the major church feasts or was obliged to come to the town to settle business matters concerning the order, or else that letter from our confessor so worried him that he feared for the health of all of the sisters. The Lord illuminated him even as He continued to draw sisters away from the choir and their labors, from their prayers and the cloister. A new sickness, an offshoot of the one that was already tormenting us, came to decimate us, one so severe and so violent that it was extremely painful to eat and even the water from the well, scant as it was, had to be cooled so as not to burn our throats.

That was the situation when the provincial finally arrived, a man of faith and talent, and in the opinion of everyone, one given to prompt decisions. He had a reputation for always beginning, like a good mason, at the bottom of the house, leaving for later the roof and the pinnacles, that is to say prayers, canonical hours, and psalms. He immediately asked to see the account books, whereupon the prioress began to sigh and lament, for everything was all mixed up, noted down in the only way that a poor woman who knew nothing of material possessions could keep books. The others, the heavenly possessions, come by themselves and prosper by themselves, as everyone knows, but those of this world here below, if people do not know how to manage them and keep account of them, very soon fly away like birds when autumn arrives. So it was that the provincial explained to her, and so it was that they spent something like half a day on the matter of other ground rents and revenues that had not been properly looked after, with the result that some of them would have to be considered as lost for the time being and the others written off altogether.

As is well known and oft-repeated, what is perishable is likely to cause grave harm to the spirit, and that was how things were with us, since we had no idea how much food should be allotted us healthy ones each day and how much appportioned to the sick ones, nor how far the grain would go, nor whether the harvest was abundant or meager. Where an old shepherd or a spendthrift prelate is in charge, the flock does not thrive and can even meet its ruin or death if matters are not put to rights in time.

Little by little, persistent man that he was, the provincial began to examine everything he found in his path, like a judge endeavoring to verify every last particular that the confessor had brought to light in his letter and denounced. He very carefully inspected the locutories especially, their double grille with closely spaced iron bars, their worn curtains, and the tiny communion window in the chapel. He had a long drawn-out conversation with his confidant, recommending that he have only the necessary dealings with us, and inquiring in minute detail as to the life and spiritual absorption of the house.

We never knew what conclusions he may have arrived at following this conversation, but he returned from it with a mournful expression on his face, saying not a word, and it was then, after that talk, that he asked to see the rest of the house, the infirmary and the cells, the granary, the stable, and even the cemetery, becoming more and more insistent as we sisters tried to dissuade him from doing so with reassuring words.

As the saying goes, the Lord found it good to forsake us; the world came tumbling down upon us, and this same Visitor, previously so kind and affable, suddenly became an antagonistic enemy. He did not retreat till he had seen the infirmary, and as our ill luck would have it, at this time one of our youngest sisters was about to leave us. Each time she closed her eyes we thought it would be forever. She had already received extreme unction, and heard the Credo as recited by the prioress. We had even placed the wax on her eyes, so certain were we that she would soon be leaving us. But the Lord so willed it that on the day of the provincial's visit she was still alive, and on becoming aware that he was approaching, she sat up on her cot and asked him to hear her confession.

The prioress tried to convince her that her soul was surely purged of all sin since she had received absolution so many times from our chaplain, that she should lie quietly and rest, otherwise she would never get well; but the sister—being of tender years, with that fear of dying that possesses the youngest ones, those whom life still looks upon with grace and favor—replied that she was certain that her grave lay open to receive her, that she would soon depart from this world in the company of others, of all the sisters who had recently been laid to rest in the court beneath the shadow of the new crosses.

The vicar asked in a loud voice how many had passed on in these last months. He also wanted to know the cause of their death, and our chaplain, as though taking sides with him, told him of our many privations and of how the sickness was destroying the house with every day that went by.

Then the two of them inspected the remainder of the flock, the vegetable garden, the kitchen, and the cells, finally coming back round to the refectory where the visit had begun.

It was not like other times. He had not asked a single question as to doubts and intentions, or new vocations. There were no words of encouragement, only a deep silence, surely the fruit of his dark and wrathful thoughts. He did not even choose to honor us by sampling the meal that the prioress had managed to prepare for him only with the greatest of difficulty, gathering together everything, sweet or salty, that was still left in the larder, along with lamb from outside the walls and produce from the convent garden. He was so absorbed in his thoughts that he did not even taste the fruit from our orchard. Nor did he deign to listen to the sisters who wasted their energies in useless speeches of welcome, in arguments and justifications, blaming everything on the drought. If it was capable of ruining so many towns and cities, they said, it was not surprising that it should come to wreak its havoc on such a poor community; but our poverty would be a mere passing thing, a gift of the Lord as the prioress said, a test by fire to which He was once again subjecting us.

But the Visitor barely listened. From time to time he consulted with our chaplain as to dates and names, facts and figures, and the chaplain deferred to the doctor, whose report was doubtless no more favorable to us.

Without taking part in the conversation or interrupting our superior, all of us, to a greater or lesser degree, regretted having thus opened the doors of our house to him, having so unthinkingly put our miseries before him, since everyone judges the faults he sees to be slight or serious in accordance with what he has been told about them beforehand. Our provincial was surely a good judge; we had always considered him to be such ever since we had known him, but the doctor's opinion must have impressed him, as had the report of our confessor, who had always gloried in ruling over us.

Whatever the reason, the memory of the empty cells, the broken roofs through which the wind roared at night, the empty granary, the walls that had tumbled down and caved in, the threatened choir, and the garden overgrown with thistles, weighed upon the mind of the vicar in whose hands the fate of the community lay, its life or death here below on this earth.

For a long time after that sudden visit, the convent was in a turmoil, awaiting its dreaded consequences. The worried, frightened sisters accused our chaplain, with contrite consciences, of having brought us an evil worse than the drought or the plagues already visited upon us. Some of them maintained that all our troubles were surely the handiwork of the Devil, bent on seeing our holy house closed, thereby driving novices and sisters to other regions and other convents. With the fear of death, which continued to decimate both our house and the districts and outskirts of the town outside our walls, our melancholy returned, for women's nature is weak—as is even that of men in such circumstances. Surely the Lord was seeking to test us by exposing us for our own good to such dangers, but at times we feared we would be unable to overcome them despite His secret judgments and despite the fact that thus far we had always had His goodness on our side.

But not all the sisters shared that view of things; the flock was deeply perturbed, some of our number tormented by the fear of death at any moment, others terrified of what might soon happen to our house and to the community. Some even went so far as to try to write to Rome behind the prioress's back, to explain that it was not right to remove us from the convent or divide us on the pretext of finding us better living conditions. Some said that our opinion should be respected, that our wishes in this matter were worth a thousand times more than a single visit, that in a word they would rather be dead, like so many sisters who lay buried in our cemetery, than alive, far from our common homeland, dearly beloved and freely chosen.

In vain the prioress, in her voice worn out by the years and the latest vicissitudes, reminded us day after day of our sacred duty to obey. With her commending it and the sisters resisting, time passed without either her cause or ours carrying the day.

My sister was the only one who took no part in those long councils that as dusk fell filled the chapter room with murmurs and voices. As though she for her part found herself at odds with everything and everyone—the state of our health, the Visitor, the prioress, and the other sisters—she never allowed her voice to be heard now that, feeling stronger and with her health definitely on the mend, she could leave her cell by herself, or the kitchen where she had begun to lend a hand as soon as she could stand on her feet, and wander about the house as she pleased. Now that our infirmary was becoming a beehive of feeble prayers once again, when our fears were at their height, she seemed renewed, as though these doubts and trials, the dire forebodings of some sisters, and the anger of the others had served her as solace in her meditations.

Since she no longer needed my help, we fell into the habit of meeting at the reservoir again, as we had in the past. There, while the others railed against the Visitor, labored at the few tasks that were still done regularly, or sought peace of mind, my sister and I talked, not as before about her health, which was clearly improved, but about that other life to be bettered, that of the convent, a subject that I would have said she had long since forgotten.

And so it was that she came to confess to me that one night some time ago, that is to say after the provincial's much-discussed visit, she had had a dream. "What was the dream?" I asked, and she answered that it had to do with the saint in the book.

I had no memory of what she was referring to. "The saint I mean is the one to whom our Lord granted the grace of His wounds, the one who bettered the fortunes of her community, thanks to her fame," she added thoughtfully.

I remembered then how attentively she had listened to me reading from that holy book that had helped to fill her empty hours and given her hope in dark moments. But, simpleton that I was, I did not see where her thoughts were taking her. Hence I asked her what the dream was that she was talking about.

"I saw the convent grow," she explained, "as much and as quickly as those beyond the wall, looking like they say the ones enjoying the favor of court do, built of rock and quarried stone, with a coat of arms on the arch, and such a great olive grove and vegetable garden, such an expanse of wheat fields belonging to us that we never again had to go without any of the necessities."

"That's a nice dream," I answered, "but it would not be happy news for us if it were to grow. We have more than enough to do just to keep our four walls from falling down without having to look after all that many leagues of land as well."

But she was not listening. She seemed, rather, to be already feeling those new walls of the house beneath her hands.

"The entire vegetable garden," she went on, "was surrounded by luxuriant trees, bearing every variety of fruit imaginable, apple trees, sweet and sour cherry trees, all of them so fertile and leafy that you could hardly see the sky between their branches."

"Sister," I said to her, "I've never seen orchards such as that here in these parts, nor any other sort of fruit than the kinds that withstand frost. And by that I mean very few kinds. But if that was what you saw in your dreams I won't gainsay you, for everyone is free to dream according to his own lights."

She also saw, she said, lovely thick grass in our cloister garth, clean water in the reservoir, not dirty and cloudy the way it was now, the kitchen full of pans and pitchers and finely shaped pots all ready for use, and the larder filled with food.

In the city, deserted in recent days because of people's fears and the lack of bread and provisions, well-being and prosperity were returning. As our natural daughter and sister, our resurrection benefited her too; a great market was held there again, just as in her best days. Once again hers was the best in the entire district, with an abundance of produce and provisions for sale, for an entire month, along with a wealth of good broadcloth, fine wool, scarlet cloth, velvet, satin, damask.

To sell these wares and others, itinerant merchants came from the four points of the compass as in bygone days, each with his assigned stall in which to display his silks, notions, or jewels: Basques with highly prized linen cloth, Portuguese with rich fabrics, and a great luxury of spices from India, silver, wax, and fish for the rigorous Lenten fasts. The duke, our lord and master, who protects and maintains our house, visibly prospered from the sales tax imposed on foreign merchants, from the fat revenues from tollhouses and city gates through which their goods passed.

But I realized full well that this was only a dream of my sister's, a ripe desire without reason or roots in our bad times. One needed only to open one's eyes to see our dilapidated adobe walls, the vault of the chapel open to the sky, the broken tiles of the refectory floor, and the death in the eyes of our sisters each time the nurse came to serve them the miserable broth that barely covered the bottom of the dish.

"That's a nice dream," I answered her, "but the truth of the matter is that our fate is in the hands of the Almighty. If it is His design that we should die, we shall very soon be embarking on the same path as the others before us."

"That cannot be the Lord's will," she replied, as though speaking to the shadow already beginning to swallow up the window. "He has tested us enough now."

She did not tell me the reason behind this strong conviction of hers; it is quite true that she never explained her thoughts to me, but I remember clearly that we remained there for a long time talking together, she very sure of herself and I all confused, not daring to ask questions, not even when she assured me that one day the king himself would come to visit us.

"The king?" I said, wondering whether her reason was disturbed again.

But my sister, like someone who no longer sees the life round about her, explained that, outside of our world, everything was possible, and would be all the more so when our house was not only large and rich, but renowned and respected even at court. And she added that at present all this was only a dream, but that from this day forward she would keep me informed of everything that would be revealed to her in the future, since very great events were about to take place. As a result of them, the house would come upon much better days and be enriched, and even I would enjoy similar changes of fortune if I were capable of keeping such revelations a secret.

The days passed without a sign of rain. Since there was no longer any wheat for the water-mills in the river, we were obliged to eat bread made of grama grass. We chopped the stems of it very fine, dried them, and after grinding them up, baked loaves of them that were worse than mediocre. One day, after summer was over, as I was on my way to the garden, I stopped to listen for signs that might be blowing in the wind. A waste of time, for no news came my way from the other side of the adobe walls, nor was there any other sound from beyond the walls save for a silence that was the sum and substance of all the silences of the earth. I peered through the lattice over the window of my cell and saw the cloudless sky far overhead, the motionless poplars, the city resting quietly on its hilltop. This time it looked even more sleepy and serene than usual, without a voice or a song, only the dim glow of distant bonfires. As the day won its round against the night, the sky gradually lowered, turning murky and ashen-colored, clinging to the earth and quite prepared to become one with it. A great smudge of smoke little by little enveloped towers and parapets, pressing in upon the town, effacing it, attacking it from above its arches and ramparts. I shall never forget seeing those towers seemingly blanketed in fog, hearing that silence like unto that of the Last Judgment, smelling that persistent odor that descended upon the outskirts of the city from on high, an odor of burnt hemp rope, of charred adobe bricks, of quicklime and mercury.

Along the king's highway, ordinarily so full of life at that hour, crowded with pack animals and people, there was only the wind, listlessly dragging along in its wake dirty stubble, heat, bits of dry thistle. The mute belfries and the dead-quiet swifts, afraid to sing or to stir, were silent both within and without the walls.

In this fashion, dispirited and uneasy, contemplating the clouds, listening to that fearful silence, neither working nor praying, we spent the morning, until the little bell at the gate rang at midday. It was our doctor, coming to pay us his usual visit, though this time a more hurried and tense one than was his habit.

Seeing the grave expression on his face, we realized that he was bringing us bad news. On his way to the infirmary he stopped for a moment to pass it on to the prioress, informing her that the last inhabitants left in the town had fled to the mountains and places close by where they thought they would be safe from the sickness. The few people who remained behind, the crippled, the disabled, or those who were simply poverty-stricken, improved their lot without let or hindrance by breaking into other people's homes and dwellings, taking for themselves whatever the more affluent townsmen had been unable to take with them. Everything else they burned, thinking that they were thereby doing away with the contagion and thus, square by square, the better districts had gone up in flames. The doctor's own house was in serious danger; after having sent his family far off, he had insisted on staying behind to protect it. The empty churches expressed better than words the true state of the town, with the dead lying everywhere unburied, without receiving their handful of earth, and the living seeking to profit in their very last hours.

The doctor's face turned graver still when he reached the infirmary. This time he barely crossed the threshold. He looked inside at those poor wasted bodies that wept without listening or understanding his words, seeking nothing now but relief from their pain. His recommendations were useless: forbidding them to eat fish when there was no fish, or advising cold meals when the heat was so stifling that even the water from the well came up thick and burning hot, like strong, viscous medicine. He was plainly contrite and dispirited, silent and dejected, like someone who does not know what remedy to offer, and perhaps asking himself when that sickness would overtake him in turn.

The prioress accompanied him as usual to the gate, at which there was likewise no sign of the faithful or of our neighbors, at which no one any longer left either tithes or alms.

"I think that this must be the end of our days," she murmured as her clumsy fingers lifted the heavy iron latch. "The first signs that the end is near."

But our doctor did not believe that this was so. He lingered for a few moments as though he were no longer in a hurry and explained how for some time now, long before the drought, the harvests had been so meager that people could no longer pay their debts and ended up in prison. The jails were full of them, and rumor had it that there was scarcely any time left for courts to hear anything but debtors' pleas and suits brought by creditors.

Some of my sisters, daughters of farm laborers, agreed with the doctor but not with the prioress, for whom man's fate depended on heaven alone. But the doctor, pressing his point, added that men of substance, merchants, and linen dealers hoarded wheat in months of abundance, selling goods on credit to be paid for later, when there was a shortage of bread, besides charging too high prices for their merchandise.

All that was true. That was how, I remembered, my parents' house had been ruined; they had remained poor, fated most of the time to fall into the same trap over and over again all year long, perpetual slaves of those who wanted grain only to resell it, thus profiting from our continual misfortunes. Our doctor was right on every score, and what was more, the prioress had forgotten Our Lord's words about the rich and the poor written in the Holy Book.

That same night two very young sisters delivered their souls to God. They were buried there in the corner of the cloister, in the forest of crosses that would soon reach the conduit from the well. They lay there beneath the lilies bordered with pointed bricks, in the well-dug earth, feeling our footsteps, and mayhap even listening to our voices. Later our contrite chaplain, like one who knows the real root of evil and how far it can reach once the reasons for it are forgotten, said to us in the forbidding darkness of the chapel:

"However terrible death may seem, as we see it swoop down upon the youngest sisters, I beseech you not to tremble, not to allow yourselves to be frightened. A short time ago one of you asked: 'Will the rest of us die too?' And I say

to you that this is a vain and idle question. Rather, lift up your hearts, for from these calamities that the Lord permits we may deduce that in no wise does He wish us to forget His memory, in order that we may be humble in adversity and understand what we owe His Majesty, beginning with our brief life here below. Life is a mere sad breath that lasts but a very short time, a light that flickers but a moment, a day that dies. Sisters, how we have forgotten the Lord, what little honor we pay Him, how irresolute our souls! For if they were filled with Him, as they should be, death would mean very little to us. Our help lies in prayer; that is the one true salvation in these black hours."

The chaplain's voice echoed off the walls in the empty church and on the other side of the grille, in our old choir that was falling to pieces. Beneath the light of the round window that divided the prioress's seat of honor in two, we had never seen the shadow of death closer at hand. Those words from beyond the iron bars seemed to be coming from the clouds, from the sky, empty now, from the very bosom of the Lord, become a stern, harsh master. The youngest sisters were weeping. They appeared to be awaiting their turn, the cold knife-edge of death, the ceremony in which we heap earth on the others, that dark mound of earth along the soil of the cloister, topped by two crossed strips of wood. They would willingly have fled far from there, from those words and those confused echoes, but faith, hope, or sheer fear kept them on their knees, praying to God that our chaplain would end his homily soon.

"Those who are not prepared," his voice went on "are perturbed and frightened at the very mention of the hour of their death, for their time and their concern have been taken up entirely by the miserable affairs of this world. This is a pernicious madness. Only those who have left all thought of worldly pleasures behind have no fear of death. Nor do they grieve for those who are already with Christ, enjoying His infinite mercy."

With the usual "amen" we soon put an end to his words, awaiting, dejected and fearful, our superior's sign allowing us to leave the chapel. As we filed out, no one said a word. It seemed to me that for the first time in many a day, such a ceremony had struck fear into our hearts, much more so than on previous occasions. Undoubtedly the reason why this was so was that before this, since it had been sisters already advanced in years who had passed on, death seemed more within the natural order of things—so cruelly do we dismiss old people—but now that it was carrying off persons born as they saw only recently to this life, we pondered whether it was not perhaps too cruel a fate to cut off their path beneath their feet in their most promising years.

The only one wholly indifferent to such fears was my sister. It was in those days that I asked myself for the first time what flesh, what blood she was made of, seeing her there, so firm and steadfast, so far removed from this world, so disinclined to engage in any sort of conversation with the others. I wondered where her thoughts were taking her, if her faith lay sleeping, her heart so little moved by charity that she shed not a single tear. But if her love was lukewarm, this was not so of her interest, above all in me. As the others wept, overcome with grief, she signaled to me that we would talk together later.

She remained absorbed in her thoughts that whole afternoon, as though her mind were somewhere else altogether,

26

contemplating the towers of the city half blotted from view by the smoke, its miserable outskirts, the blind belfries of the other convents. What might our sister nuns of other houses be doing in the face of such dire events? They had fled, most likely; it could well be that they had abandoned the city like everyone else, seeking refuge in more propitious holdings of the sort that belonged to great, well-to-do orders.

We, on the other hand, were obliged to remain there where we were, awaiting who knew what other calamity that was the brother of death, clinging to our faith and our prayers.

All during this day, that dream my sister had told me of kept coming back to my mind. I too saw the city on the hilltop full of life and brightly gleaming, as in better times, and pilgrims and travelers hastening to our gate seeking bread and blessings.

I too dreamed of the arrival of our lord and master the king, imagining the messages he would send announcing his arrival, what his voice, his manner, his person would be like. I saw him entering beneath the main arch of the wall, under his golden canopy, surrounded by footmen, church dignitaries, royal cavalrymen, dismounting before our gate, clothed in splendor, swathed in rich tapestries and fine fabrics, crowned with laurel in honor of such an important occasion.

Our now-flourishing community would come out to receive him in the cloister garth and the new prioress would come forward to kiss his august hand. A solemn Te Deum would follow, and as the voices of the novices resounded the chapel would seem like the antechamber of heaven, amid the fragrance of incense, the sound of hymns sung in perfect harmony, and their warm echoes.

But such dreams were fleeting ones, lasting only the time

it took to sweep a flight of stairs, to scrub the tiled floor of the refectory, or wash the nightdresses of a few ailing sisters. They returned only at hours of meditation, at once stubborn and sweet, especially at night, more powerful then than ever.

And it was at night, when I was alone in my cell with Our Lord, that my sister came to pay me an urgent visit, as though she were bearing an important message. At that hour of the night, I was allowing my soul to rest, occupying it only in prayer, that great consolation for the loneliness of love and for the great heartache that comes from the lack of it. At such times no remedy is satisfactory, for the sister who loves greatly does not accept advice or admonitions from the others, but only another love that will relieve the pain. Hence I demonstrated my gratitude for her visit with great signs of affection, hoping that that night at least my sorrows and desolation would find a remedy and her presence bring me solace in my wretchedness. But again, as earlier in the refectory, I fancied that her face had a distant, pensive look about it. Seeing that serious expression, I was immediately disheartened, ready merely to listen, to obey, caught between two lighted fires, between the one who loves, that is to say the one who gives everything, and the one who is prepared to receive that gift.

When we proceeded to give each other the kiss of peace as at other times, her mouth lingered long on my cheek. I noticed then that she was trembling, and therefore I asked her:

"What is this, sister? Are you ill again?"

But she did not answer, as though racked by terrible anguish. Her body felt as though it were about to break, her hands were ice-cold, and her breath next to my mouth as searing as that other wind that had now enveloped the city and its walls, making them gleam in the darkness like the glow of a red-hot ember.

A moment later she stepped away from me, and wrapping her cape about her, walked over to the window overlooking the patio, listening attentively to the sounds coming from outside. Seeing her draw away from me I was deeply hurt, even sadder and more downcast than before. Love, you are a wicked enemy, bringing such sore trials, such sudden starts of fear to those who seek out another's heart so as to weep and love till sated!

I who would have given my life to save her, to raise her spirits as on so many other occasions in the past, was overcome by doubts now as I waited for her to explain the reason for her dejection, fearing that by worsening her health the Lord had begun to punish us for things that I shall tell of later. And then the thought came to me that He was incapable of showing such cruelty toward such poor creatures as we, women with no solace save work and prayer, with no other reward save their great wretchedness. He would not want to deprive us of our only comfort and delight, of that love capable of curing the wounds in our souls, to punish us for misdeeds at once so sweet and so secret. The Lord would be willing to allow us to continue to enjoy such sweet pleasure, such joyful torment amid so many cruel and serious hardships. For what would He gain by depriving us of it? He Who so loved us must know of what clay we are fashioned, what love does and undoes, holding as we know the heavens and the earth in its sway.

29

My sister's voice suddenly erased these thoughts from my mind.

"I've come to seek your help."

I was I who remained silent now. Finally I asked:

"Is it something that must be done immediately, at this late hour?"

"It's nothing of any great importance; on the contrary, it's something quite trivial. It will only take a moment."

"Tell me what it's all about. I'll do everything I can to help"

"I'll tell you later."

But to judge from her impatience, her alertness to every sound coming from the cloister, her reason for coming to me did not appear to be all that trivial. She came back over to where I was standing.

"Come with me."

And only half willingly, I picked up my cape, and throwing it over my shoulders, I followed along behind her, after first carefully pulling the door of my cell shut.

Outside, the cloister with its dark arches and frightened rosebushes was dead silent, as though the moonlight were a blanket of snow. From beyond the walls there came the lonely hoot of owls, a bell ringing somewhere far off in the distance, the sough of the wind on the hilltop, and the sighing of the cloud-swept sky. The two of us made our way along in the same manner, out feet barely touching the ground, like two shadows flying through the air. Halfway to our destination, there came thundering through the air from the city the solemn voice of its great bell. It was as though I were hearing it for the first time, such was the state that the sound of it left me in, petrified, seeking sanctuary in the shadow of the arches as its echoes lingered. Then finally the breath returned to my body, the blood to my heart, and the two of us hurried on.

Once we had reached her cell, my sister ordered me to sit down. My weary bones collapsed on the blanket covering her bed, as mean and shabby as the pallets of all the rest of us. We both fell silent once again, she standing there listening attentively in the darkness and I, her slave, awaiting a word from her to enlighten me in the midst of that pitch blackness. Only after some time did she abruptly break the silence to ask me if I still loved our house.

An idle question. Was there any reason to doubt that I loved those four walls, ruined as they were, worn away by the rain, cracked by the sun, felled by the wind? It was not that question that I had been expecting, but rather some small sign of affection or compassion, a single word that would serve to revive in me that flame that by her presence or her aloofness she either kindled or extinguished.

"And what about me? Do you still love me a little?"

A self-assured way of beginning. She was intimately aware of my affection for her, my eagerness to follow her as far as she wished or would consent to. I still loved her, a very great deal, each and every day, despite her silences and her illness. I was still flesh of her flesh, voice of her voice, breath of her breath as I had been the very first time, back in the spring, long before the drought, when we first became acquainted with each other and the city that rose with the sun seemed like a golden paradise with its solemn towers and its bright-red stones. Our pledge to each other still held good, despite her detachment. Hence I answered her in tears that my affection for her was till as steadfast as ever, was ever with me, kept vigil in the night, still found its nurture in me as in our best, most resolute hours.

But she asked the same question again.

How to explain? What to add, after so many nights that the two of us had spent together, consoled, as one? Our love for each other had gone too far; we had traveled its path of pleasures and pains too long to turn back, to stop now, to doubt as we had in the first days. Which of us would be capable of giving up now, despite risks or tears? Not I surely, still ready to give rather than to receive, the servant of love, of my sister's body. Not I, ever and always prepared to follow her lead in everything, in happy days as in sad ones, in her ardor as in her coldness, and mayhap even in her sins. Not I, with no will of my own, altogether hers body and soul, light of her light and shadow of her shadow, she without whom the world seemed to me a cross too heavy for my little strength to bear.

It was in words such as these that I answered her question, awkwardly, hurriedly, and she looked at me once again with the same expression in her eyes as always. She thereupon wanted to know what I was prepared to do to prevent the downfall of our house.

"Everything," I answered.

What could I do? What could the two of us do? It was quite true that neither of us came from families of low estate. It was perhaps for that very reason that we very soon became friends and sought each other out. Our parents were not people in dire want like those of so many other novices taken in by our poor order; at one time they had owned lands and vineyards, and even though they did not wear silver or jewels or coral necklaces, or silks and rich fabrics at fiestas and weddings, they were noble families who had come down in the world by borrowing money and selling their property to pay their debts, and had not fallen so low as to hire themselves out to work for others, much less beg for a living. My sister and I came from families of much higher estate; we realized this immediately, the moment we first set eyes on each other one autumn afternoon in the shadow of the cloister. Time went by, and soon our friendship ripened, bringing love in its wake shortly after. But the love that moves heaven and mountains would be of little use to us now that the time had come to put the future of the house to rights.

"Does the fate of the order by some chance lie in our hands?" I asked her.

My sister nodded. Then she came to me and took my hands, friendly once again, the frown on her face gone. She seemed her former self once more, but to my unhappiness, even though we were together again, her thoughts were still far away, beyond the walls of the cell, beyond the warm, tender semidarkness, beyond my affection for her. She recounted to me once again the dream she had had for many nights now, the one about the abbess who, her hands and feet touched by God's grace, had caused her convent to prosper.

It was plain to see that her head was still going round and round, but what she was concerned about was not the story of the saint but our future, whether or not we too would be capable of saving our house in like manner.

"The fate of the order depends on us, on our faith and courage. Why should we be less favored than other orders?"

I sat there looking at her, unable to tell whether resentment was blinding her or whether this was another dream like the one she had had on so many nights, but she returned insistently to the subject, like someone who already has a definite plan in mind, carefully thought through and lacking only in some sort of help that was certain to be forthcoming. This was the reason for her visit that night, for her vague silences and her constant watchful expression. But by her own efforts alone, or even if the two of us acted together, it was impossible for me to imagine where we would find enough alms in such hard and trying times, with the city empty and our benefactor absent, at court as usual. Things would have been entirely different in years past, when bread was baked in the city each morning, when patterned silks were woven to adorn beds, wool fabrics of all sorts were made, and the king's highway could be seen to be crowded with porters bearing great loads of provisions, of oil, fish, and wine, on their way to important markets. In those days our benefactor used to appear for Easter with a handful of ducats which, if they were not enough to cover all our needs, at least helped to relieve a little of the burden on our meager treasury, badly depleted because so many poor novices without dowries had been taken into the house.

"Back then, that was possible, but not now," I answered, after reminding her of all this. "Furthermore, we are not saints like the one in your dream. Never, so far as I can recall, has anything outside the natural order of things ever happened in this house, anything any different from what we know has happened in so many other houses like this one."

"That is what I wished to speak to you about this night."

"It may well be that the Lord will look with favor upon us some day."

"The Lord doesn't hear us."

She remained silent after saying this, and her tone of voice had been such that I was frightened: somewhere between solemn and threatening, with a determination that surely had been slowly maturing during all those long nights.

"The Lord doesn't hear us," she repeated. "It is quite evident that He has forsaken us. Our prayers avail us nothing if He decimates us each month. Soon we shall all be lying beneath that many more crosses, in a corner of the cloister."

"What can we do? His designs do not depend on us. All we can do is pray and resign ourselves."

"Certainly not. I for my part refuse to resign myself."

Her anger grew and I trembled even more, fearing that the sound of her voice and her arguments would carry beyond the walls of the cell. I had never seen her in such a state, nor until then ever heard words from her lips that sounded to my ears more like heresy, the fruit of a brief fit of rage, than like the holy wrath of God. I wanted to make her see how much pride lay in them, how they were merely passing rancors against Our Lord God, an invention of the Devil, who never stops trying to butt his way in, from horns to tail, whenever a person's soul seems to fall prey to anxieties. She had best seek out a confessor, and unburdening herself with humility, tell him of the state in which she found herself. He might well show her the light with regard to everything that was happening. But my sister refused. She said that she was able to save the convent alone if in the end I did not agree to help her. It was useless to ask her how I could assist her. She thereupon became as aloof and cold as before, letting me leave her cell without giving me the kiss of peace, her manner pensive and distant once again.

The following morning brought us yet another sudden unexpected event. This time it was a strange procession that began at daybreak, accompanied by a wild pealing of bells. They tumbled back and forth as in better times, that of the cathedral deep-voiced and ceremonious, the closer ones lively and joyous, the echoes of some of them merging with the brief chiming of the others.

The more curious of the sisters stood watching at the latticed windows, eagerly awaiting this new turn of events that would relieve our hours of tedium. It might turn out to be a visit from the bishop, or the passing of a royal cortege on the way to heaven only knew where, or the arrival of our benefactor, something that would be most surprising at such a time as this, what with sickness raging within our walls and the plain and the city empty.

The sun was directly overhead now, and yet there was no sign of life as yet on the highway, nor had the main gate of the city been thrown wide open. Everything remained the same as before: the city dead silent and the bells pealing. From time to time they stopped ringing, as though weary. Little by little, one after the other, they fell silent, only to begin after a time to all ring out at once again, louder than ever, thereby scattering both our thoughts and the jackdaws.

At midday we discovered the reason for this din. The portress descended from the bell-tower to tell us that a procession was coming our way along the road from the hermitage on the plain. Shortly thereafter, we caught sight of it, split up into two parts, coming around from behind the walls with their crosses held on high, with all those whom death had spared dragging along behind. There they came, with their sores and songs, trying to drive away the drought by dint of fervor and curses. They cursed the sun, the bright clean sky, the wind that refused to drive the clouds before it, the dust, the parched ears of grain, then suddenly burst forth in prayer, though heaven alone knew whether they were calling on God or on the rainfall that was proving to be so elusive.

Closer now as they passed by our latticed windows, we could see them, with the skin stuck to their tortured flesh and cilices even more cruel than ours, some of them bearing their cross on their shoulders, others with flayed backs and blood oozing from their feet which the dust of the fields had turned into crusts of mud. No one, not even the lay-sister portress, recognized their faces; none of us remembered ever having seen them before. They were like an evil flock, a wicked brotherhood of the Devil despite their crosses and their hymns, the advance guard of the Universal Judgment come to wipe us off the face of the earth.

Seeing them walking past, falling, staggering, shouting to heaven, we asked ourselves how the Lord could permit such abominations, why He did not confound them there and then in a lightning flash of wrath, as He had the moneychangers in the temple, as He had Saul on the road to Damascus.

As we learned later, they were going about from town to town, from city to city, in ever-growing numbers despite the fact that they had been excommunicated. They continued on their way night and day, across the plain, weak and battered, all mingled together promiscuously, men and women, until some charity, convent, or household took pity on them and gave them a bit of barley, a handful of grain to lift to their mouths.

We also learned that from time to time, in the night, they celebrated their rites and their sabbats, on which occasions they experienced more often than not ecstasies and visions that should have earned them the sanbenito and cone-shaped hat of heretics condemned by the Holy Office. As the prioress assured us, they were not saintly people or even followers of Our Mother Church, nor did their sacrifices and penitences exorcise the evil that had befallen Christians, as they maintained; they were, rather, depraved animals whinnying with lust in order to blot out the memory of their wicked deeds.

That must have been so, for until far into the night, in the warmth of bonfires that lighted up the pasturelands of the plain, their shouts and songs could be heard, and it was plain to us that theirs were not voices raised in piety or lament, but rather in celebration of heinous union and lascivious pleasure.

As simple women living a life of sanctity in the house, many sisters did not understand the meaning of those miserable voices. They had never heard nor witnessed such activities, nor did they understand why Our Lord God, after visiting so many calamities and misfortunes upon us, should now be pleased to discountenance us with the terrible sin of the flesh.

None of us slept on those nights. Not even my sister, who declared:

"God permits all these offenses so as to humiliate us."

I did not understand the meaning of her words. I thought that if Satan were thus permitted to wreak his evil, thereby testing our own virtue, in the end our souls would be damaged.

"They will not be all that greatly harmed. On the contrary, they will thereby be saved."

"And how will that come about, sister?"

"Through love," she answered me. "More than all other

acts, it supplements the virtues that can be attained by following the usual path."

It was through love that she always won me over. I knew this well, after so many days and nights together in the semidarkness of her cell till dawn broke. Her warm breath, her trembling hands, her eyes next to my mouth always won me over, took the place within me of everything that troubled me or lingered in my mind during the day, everything I listened to or took pleasure in, the soft breeze at dawn caressing me, the sound of the birds singing, the soft touch of her flesh against my flesh.

She was well aware of this; she knew the path that in the end would make me forget my fears, and as on that first occasion, so well planned, prepared with such firm purpose, zeal, and cleverness, in like manner now she obliged me to help her carry out her designs. This was days after that perverted troop had continued on its way, leaving behind it, like worms, a despicable slime of filth and muck.

Chapter Two

S HE sought me out as on so many other nights, and this
time she began by asking me what I thought about
those people who had left us a short time before. I replied
that they seemed to me to be depraved and lustful sorts, more
attached to earthly pleasures than to heaven's gifts, deserving
to appear before the Holy Tribunal, to have a good taste of
starvation rations and come to know the feel of the lash. But
many of them were wandering about announcing supposed
revelations, preaching the union of man and woman in order
to bring into the world a new race of prophets. And what
was more: they assured their hearers that humans committed
no sin if such a thing came to pass once they reached a state
of ecstasy in which, the senses being annihilated, their powers
of reason left them, since the body alone could know no sin
or guilt.

"Well then, we will carry out our plan in ecstasy." And
taking a small knife out from under the folds of her habit,
my sister held it out to me in silence.

"What is this for?" I asked before taking it.

"To save the house."

"With a weapon as small as this?"

"With this weapon and my hands."

She held them out to me and I kissed them, asking myself if I would be capable of wounding them and she capable of withstanding the pain of the knife-thrust. She explained to me very clearly how, once her flesh was mortified, someone would soon spread the word that her wounds were the work of Our Lord. People would throng to the house and once the drought and the sickness became less severe, our fame would spread to the court itself.

I trembled once more. All that brought back to my mind words of the prioress long ago, when on rare occasions she would speak to us of false prophets and new heresies. Deceiving the order, the city, and the world beyond the walls was a grave sin, even if, as my sister desired, Our Lord were to grant us the grace of ecstasy. Committing the deed, allowing it to flourish, to grow, lying day after day, earning fame and fortune even though it be for the good of the convent seemed to me to be more than a transgression against dogma: it was the sin of pride. How could Our Lord forgive us? How would we be able to receive Him each day, to feel Him in our bodies defiled by falsehood?

But my sister always had answers to my questions, as though she had long been planning the step we were about to take. No one would know the truth. The wounds would last as long as necessary. Then, once the house was saved and the bad times were over, she herself would reveal the truth to the chaplain and both our souls would be redeemed after we had done severe penance.

"They may discover the truth before that."

My sister looked at the sky beyond the window, rent by flashes of lightning far off in the distance.

"Everyone sees fantastic things and strange apparitions these days. Haven't you heard tell of the bells of Velilla?"

"I know only those of the city and those of this house."

"Haven't you heard talk of the miraculous bell?"

"I've never heard tell of it."

"Well, I can tell you that it peals all by itself, without anyone laying a hand on it, when some misfortune is about to happen. Deaths of kings, grave disasters, wars, or plagues."

"Like now?"

She did not answer, and merely kept peering outside. Perhaps she was searching for some special sign there amid that confused jumble of lights, some sign that would allow her to divine her good or bad luck. I told her that that book and her sickness had made her a different person.

"That is true. I know now what happens in communities where such things happen, where stigmata and nuns chosen by the Lord appear. Not like our house, where all we know how to do is pray and hope. Alms rain down on those other houses. They are never poor. It is not necessary to divide them or close them because they are unable to pay their ground-rent or because they sometimes lack a handful of ducats."

"So you think then that they are going to separate us?"

"Undoubtedly; if the Visitor's report is as I fear, they will divide the community up between other houses that can take us in."

"Perhaps we'll be sent to the same one."

"Only the Lord knows."

43

"Or mayhap they'll separate us."

I looked at the knife for the first time, so small and so bright. I asked myself how I could defend our union by means of such a tiny weapon, and trying it on my own flesh, I exclaimed:

"No matter what happens, I will not abandon you."

"Well then, hurry up, let's begin this minute."

She lay down on her bed, leaving the arm closest to me outside the bedclothes. I hesitated, so great were my misgivings, my fear still. The knife trembled, afraid to plunge itself in that soft, sweet, affectionate flesh. Instead of wounding it I began to kiss it, beginning with her fingers, then following the path of her pale veins till both of us were lying on the bed, united and vanquished, on top of the miserable quilt. It was a dream like so many others in the past, dead now, in which love and will lost themselves till daybreak, when the two of us, locked in each other's arms, trembling, consoled, each seeking the other, the hurried pounding of our blood making us one, saw the light arrive like a hostile messenger who would snatch away and carry off with him the sweet hours of the night. It was like enjoying an agony eagerly desired, like wax that melts and dies in the heat of the flame, like facing the world and sating ourselves with passion forever, a glorious madness, a splendid folly, an abundance of true carnal pleasure.

It was all that. And it all happened again that night. Then finally, become myself once more, having recovered my senses, I took the knife without further hesitation and plunged the tip of it into the palms of her hands.

When the blood spurted forth, uniting us once again, intoxicated with love and folly, she whispered softly:

44

"Gently, sister. Try not to let your hand tremble."

When the blood dried, leaving on her skin a delicate tracery of red spiderwebs, the two of us rose to our feet with panting breath, bathed in sweat, thirsty and distant. I suddenly felt the touch of her lips from the nape of my neck to my throat, seeking my lips, and as her mouth besieged mine, I did not experience a growing happiness within me as I always had before, but instead a great anxiety, that even in my worst moments I had never felt. It was as though in that common undertaking I was in the same position as the poor, who neither win nor lose, whose only role is to obey.

In any event, this was no time for regrets. Alone and parted from my sister, where would I go? With whom would I share my loneliness? Without her the house seemed to me a vale of tears, sad and empty. She was for me my cause and reason for being, the gardener of my secret garden, the salt of my earth, the flowing spring of my body. So I took the knife that she had forgotten, as though leaving behind the memory of her crime, and hid it in my bosom as I headed for the door.

"You keep it," she said to me. "If it is in your cell they won't suspect anything."

"I hope not," I answered from the threshold. "And may the Lord have pity on us."

It was the Lord's will to test us once more through the death of the youngest sisters. The next one was a most obedient servant of His, so faithful in her devotions and so virtuous that to my way of thinking she did not even set foot in Purgatory. Her merits were surely more than sufficient. Another one, however, died without making confession, suddenly carried off by the sickness as though Satan did not want to lose time. As we took her body downstairs to bury it with the same ceremony as all the others, I asked myself if God's goodness would save her, if He would keep her soul from being lost forever, if mine would meet the same fate. I went about in consant fear at every moment, at times determined to hasten to our confessor, at times ready to kneel down before all the sisters, proclaiming my fault and my sin or else flee far from the others in the night, to a place where no one could possibly know who I was. But the Lord, or my sister's blind determination, prevailed over my feeble will and hence my life went on as before, as I awaited the consequences of the grave step we had taken.

They very soon saw the light of day, only a few days later, right there in the choir, where long ago my sister had fallen into a dead faint the first time. This time too it was at matins, and again we were singing half-asleep, remembering in fear and trembling our sisters most recently carried off in the flower of life to Him who giveth it and taketh it away. Our voices, raised in tenuous gray columns of breath there in the semidarkness, had a sorrowful sound as the gaze of all of us turned again and again to the stalls that were empty now. We found no comfort in our prayers, merely a bitter sadness, a profound and anxious unease that when it came time to take Communion made us burst into tears that lasted till we began our daily tasks.

I often asked myself at the time why my sister was hanging back after having forced me to take action so hastily, what opportunity it was that she was awaiting, until one night when, as dawn was just about to break, she suddenly fell headlong to the floor.

As before, a throng of nuns and coifs immediately surrounded the sister who had just fallen. For a moment, seeing her lying there completely motionless, as though dead, I wondered whether her faint might not be genuine, for her fall had been a violent one and her head had struck the wooden floor with a resounding thud.

At that point matins had just ended. Some of the sisters fought to carry her out of the chapel, and the others to raise her to her feet again, as the prioress made her way to her side with great difficulty amid all the arms and skirts. Finally they carried her inert body to the main choir stall, more spacious and unobstructed, and let in a bit of damp night air to see if that cold draft would bring her round. I lingered behind, apart from the others, waiting to see what would happen, still racked with doubts as to whether this was another attack of her old sickness or whether this dead faint was an act of sheer deception, like the wounds.

Whatever the reason, my sister was reluctant to return to this world. The moment her head was raised, her face drooped on her chest like a dead weight again; it was no use to hold her upright, to try to make her walk, or even to hoist her bodily to her feet. The doctor was summoned once again, but since he was not expected to arrive immediately, nor indeed was there any certainty that he would be coming any time soon, the prioress ordered two of the strongest sisters to raise her to her feet gradually and help her back to her cell and her bed, where she could rest those legs of hers as weak as blades of oats.

They were thus trying to lift her up when the youngest of her helpers, catching sight of her hands, gave a stifled cry. Immediately the others came running, including the prioress who had been about to leave and now retraced her steps.

The wounds that I had made were there, but larger now, swollen and ashen-colored, in the middle of the palms of her hands, as though born of her own flesh, without a sign of a knife-thrust or any traces of cuts.

I myself was assailed by doubts. I asked myself if those marks were my handiwork or proof of the Lord's grace, an answer to our prayers. Even I was not able to recognize in them our mutual fraud, that deception that was the work of both of us, as the others tried their best to fathom their real nature.

"They're wounds; just look at how they're bleeding."

"They may have already been there that other time when she fell to the floor."

"That's true, I saw them then, when she was dead to the world the way she is now."

The prioress also looked at them closely, though no one could tell whether she believed or disbelieved that they were real wounds. She seemed to be unable to make up her mind, perhaps because of her failing eyesight, and her words were equally hesitant when it came time to answer the other sisters' questions. She merely murmured: "Who knows?"— doubtless thanking God that the end of her responsibilities as prioress of our house was close at hand. But the sisters following along behind her raised a flurry of questions:

"Why shouldn't the Lord have chosen our convent?"

"Is there any reason for it to be favored less than others?"

"It is our duty to obey His counsels, not to judge them."

48

"But are they real wounds or not?"

"Raise the sister to her feet and take her to her cell; and let us have done with all this talk."

"But Mother, what if they are real ones? Will you send word to the provincial?"

"Time will tell. It may well be that in a few days they will disappear like so many others."

"May the Lord will otherwise!"

"Who knows?" There was a grave expression on her aged face as she left the chapel, leaning on her old cane to lead her flock before her.

"Isn't it true that such a thing has never happened here in this house before?"

"No, not within my memory," she deigned to reply to yet another question.

"May the Lord grant that they be real ones!"

"In my opinion," she concluded as she made her way to my sister's cell, "these are times that are too trying. In previous days it was the Lord's will to test us in our misfortunes. It may well be that now it is His will to measure us by our vanities."

Those wounds, poisoned and ashen-colored as they now were, nonetheless brought the community new hope, above and beyond the silence of our superior. For some of the sisters, they were a blessing from the Lord who had thus singled us out for His favor; for others they were a sign that something extraordinary would happen: mayhap the end of the drought and of the sicknesses that were destroying us. And for all the sisters something with which to fill those threatening and empty days, a new faith that would save us, and along with us the wheat for bread and the towns, the land, and the olive trees. Suddenly our destiny lay there, in the hands of my sister, who spoke not a word, who regained her senses, opened her eyes for brief moments, and then closed them once more with an otherworldly expression on her face.

Our doctor did not appear for some time. Perhaps he had been reunited with his family and forgotten both the town and our house, thinking only of his own health, of the health of his loved ones, hoping that the sickness would go away, or prepared like so many others to depart for even more distant places. The days passed one by one as we worked in the vegetable garden, but neither I nor the other sisters were calm enough or patient enough to keep our minds on cultivating the scraggly rows of kohlrabi, the only sustenance left us and the one ingredient that went into our miserable soups.

Half in terror, half in ecstasy, torn between my fears and my hopes for the glory of the house, I could see it growing, the way my sister had seen it grow in her dreams. I felt myself to be the tender of rich fields and orchards, all ours as far as the eye could see, I could see our reservoir brimming over, hear the murmur of the wind in the branches of our myrtles and cherry trees, the happy tread of our teams of oxen and our herds. I could see those scrub lands, seared now by the sun and ravaged by winter's hard freezes, become pleasing and flourishing expanses, green, red, gold, producing an abundance of bread, wine, and oil, surrounded by a great flock of the faithful, and at the same time I could see the refectory larger and more spacious, full of as great a number of sisters as the cloister and the choir.

And at last our doctor came, not with bad news, at least not with any worse news than what we already knew, his manner at once grave and diffident. He was a man well acquainted with life, toughened by the many deaths he had seen on the battlefields where he had learned his profession. He was a married man who lived an upright life, and in addition to other virtues and talents, he possessed intelligence and learning easily the equal of that of the wisest surgeons.

He could have left the town, he sometimes assured us in his chats with us, but the wish to prosper did not trouble his sleep, nor did the life at court appeal to him.

At times he impressed me as being too humble and at other times too proud, as though both tendencies were at war within him, with each of them emerging victorious at one moment or another, depending on circumstances.

Hence I asked myself what sort of humor he would be in as he visited my sister, what his final verdict would be, whether he would ferret out her falsehood. I saw him arrive and fell in behind him like most of the other sisters, halting at times so that the prioress wouldn't spy us. We followed along in his footsteps collecting crumbs of words, shadows of gestures, scraps of facial expressions, pretending to be busy at tasks that we had already finished in the portico, at the entrance, in the cloister, on the stairway, begging each other not to make a sound as we walked down the passageways leading to her cell.

He seemed to be eager to hear about her case, to shed light upon it and drive away specters that in his opinion were of little consequence, since according to what he said this would not be the first time that an entire convent had suffered from that sort of visions. He himself had not encountered prodigies of this sort, but he had heard clerics and chaplains talk of other similar miracles which, once they were denounced, turned out to be mere illusions, if not childish deceptions.

Hearing his words, seeing him about to enter my sister's cell, my distress returned and tears came to my eyes. On the one hand, I wanted to serve her in any and every way possible, as tender proof of my love and my courage; yet on the other hand I was afraid of opposing the will of God, of serving Satan through our sin, of introducing his seed into our house. What would become of me, what would become of my sister, if in the end our doctor decreed that the wounds were fraudulent? Where would they take us? What could we say in our defense? What would the prisons of the world be like?

We finally reached her cell, the prioress tapped gently on the door, and with an Ave Maria she and the doctor went inside. We saw my sister sit up in bed, greet the doctor, and then, upon a sign from him, show him her hands. The doctor took them, looked at them and palpated them very intently, saying not a word, turned them over, closed them to see if they hurt her. She denied several times that they did, and the doctor looked at the prioress every so often with a dubious expression on his face. We were all standing silently outside the door, following the scene through the chinks in it, describing it to the sisters who were waiting expectantly behind us, trying to hear the words being spoken inside, very few of which reached our ears.

"In my opinion, they look more like wounds than sores," he murmured.

"And what is the difference?"

"A wound is an injury that causes a break in the skin. It can be caused by any sort of sharp object. The odd thing is there is one in both her hands. They can also be caused by an excess of work: splitting wood, digging, pruning, a continuous wearing away of the skin, a splinter or a thorn not promptly removed. But even so it is difficult to explain why there should be two of them."

"Like Our Lord's wounds."

"And also like those of so many that are fraudulent. Sores, on the other hand, come from some local corruption, some internal cause."

My sister was not saying a word. Seen from a distance, there between the doctor and the prioress, she appeared to have no strength left, lying with her eyes closed, as though about to depart from this world. From time to time I forgot the reason and cause of all those deliberations that were taking place in the cell, as though the stigmata were genuine ones and not merely holes oozing blood that were the work of my own hands. My uneasiness grew by the moment as the prioress's questions about the wounds became more insistent and the doctor evaded them. Finally, feeling hounded, he agreed to prescribe a medicine for her that might serve to heal them over or at least prevent them from becoming bigger.

"But what if they are genuine?" the old woman asked implacably. "Wouldn't trying to heal them be to oppose the Lord's desires?"

The doctor, already heading for the door, halted, a shadow dancing in his eyes.

"If they heal, sister, it's because there's nothing supernatural about them. Let us allow time itself to decide."

The two of them left the cell, so oblivious to everything but the matter at hand that they barely saw us; the prioress carefully closed the door behind her like someone jealously hiding a treasure or concealing a dangerous threat from the eyes of others. The doctor was already heading down the passageway, looking thoughtful after his own fashion, with the short, steady stride of those accustomed to making good use of their strength. The prioress took some time to catch up with him, leaning on her cane with the silver handle, a memento of other, better days. Just before they reached the cloister, they halted to listen to our voices at their backs.

"Do we have a saint, Mother?"

It was one of the youngest sisters who, with the impulsiveness of youth and of simple souls, had blurted out the question that none of the others dared ask.

"What are all of you doing here? What are you waiting for?"

But not a one of us budged. It was as though we were forcing her by our very presence to give the young sister a definite answer.

"Mother . . . tell us the truth . . . ."

"What I shall tell you is to go on about your business." And she followed along behind the doctor.

When I saw the two of them walking off, both still in doubt and far from satisfied, thereby giving my sister and me another brief respite, I felt a little less anxious. We were safe for a few weeks still. It might well be that before the next visit my sister's wounds would disappear, and that fear of another severe attack might vanish as well, thus taking us back to our days of love, far from grievous troubles and terrors.

The days pass; there is no news from the city, nor from the court. The threat of autumn approaches, announced by the moss color of late afternoon, the skies rent by shadows of pale knives. The city wall seems farther away each dawn, the sole sign of life the flight of a falcon, the noisy wheeling of jackdaws. My sister still does not leave her cell, so far from us and yet at the same time present in our conversations and in our prayers. Everything—silence and supplications—revolves about her, is addressed to her, shrouds her, and transforms her there beyond the door barred to all save the prioress and the lay sister who brings her supper to her before dusk falls.

Nor is there any news of her. It is as though she is no longer my sister, she who so often sought me out in the past. Her kingdom is no longer my kingdom, her heart belongs to her alone, her hands no longer become one with my hands. Will our love perchance end now, because of this double sin plotted, planned, committed because of that very love? At times I am moved by a profound desire to abandon the entire undertaking, to make a full confession to the chaplain. Rather than her pretending to be a saint and giving herself false stigmata, we should let things be, even if this were to mean being humiliated and separated. God help us, what trials and tribulations and torments love brings on, what dangers, how much honor it demands that we risk! Yet who could resist its invitation!

I have begun to be overcome by a sadness that I can neither keep from speaking of, nor conceal, that fills me with contrition, especially as darkness falls. I know no rest, above all when I lie in my bed and sleep will not come. It is a great sorrow to me, moreover, to see myself occupied during the day by tasks that obedience demands but that have nothing to do with the undertaking that truly matters to me, that lifts my spirits and sustains me. My will is entirely hers still, though heretofore it was she who guided it and now it is aimless and defenseless; the two of us apart, separated, free; I willingly acknowledge that I am incapable of going on by myself, of acting without my friend and companion at my side. The convent, the sickness, the drought are of no importance to me if I compare them to the loneliness I feel without her; not even the faces that from time to time appear at the gate begging for a few mouthfuls of soup move me to compassion. What do such dire trials matter compared to my own? What does anyone know of what it means to die as I am dying, to fall to pieces, to feel that each new day that dawns is yet another calvary? One who suffers pain all alone lives and suffers in his flesh and blood a torment as deep and cruel as the one that made Our Lord, abandoned by all, tremble and shiver with fear.

If I were not afraid of breaking the thread of my destiny, if I were not afraid of the other sisters, of the Holy Office, of the wrath of the chaplain and the prioress, I would not be able to keep silent about that truth we share, but that truth, those dark blood stains are the one tie that unites us, the reminder of our only hope of living together once again those tender dawns, that fire of love that still flickers within me, suffocates me, tortures me.

Better to remain silent, to lie awake, to pray. The Lord who is almighty will know how to extricate me from this painful dilemma, to unite us again as in days gone by, to banish from my memory my sister's foolish signs of disdain and these endless days awaiting the next visit of the doctor.

The Lord then came to confound me in the following manner: my father fell ill, and because news such as that soon becomes known, I wished to see him, since it might be for the last time, in view of the ailments that his advanced years and great hardships were heaping upon him. The prioress was kind enough to grant me permission to make the journey, and so it was that I spent several days awaiting a cart willing to take me in that direction. Bitter days, and nights even worse, my soul with neither guide nor spiritual exercise of any sort, spent wondering whether my eagerness to leave the convent was motivated more by my desire to flee from my sister than by that of seeing my father in his last days, whether her abandonment of me was more than I could bear, whether my pride was capable of disguising itself in the trappings of charity and devotion.

The others, seeing me flee from them, hearing me weep in corners here and there, asked me why I was so unhappy, and I lied, feigning a great impatience to be off, until one day the chance to leave finally presented itself and the date of my departure was set.

I was given as my companion for the journey that lay sister who sometimes looked after the kitchen, a dull-witted but cheerful creature, calm and serene, ready and willing to face up to any sort of contretemps. Doubltess the prioress thought that she would serve me as a guardian angel. And so on the appointed day the two of us left the house behind us, she with great satisfaction and I with my head in a whirl.

As the dust blotted out behind me the trees of the orchard, our humble belfry, I felt more acutely than ever the thorn of my loneliness, the invisible memory of that sister who at that moment may or may not have been secretly watching our departure from behind the latticed window of her cell. Her ingratitude, her indifference hurt me a hundred times more now as I pictured her in my mind there in her cell, silent, motionless, on her way to becoming a saint.

My companion meanwhile did her best to raise my spirits. "This will soon pass," she said to me, thinking of the state my father was in. "In just a week this bad moment will be only a memory." But I knew full well that the Devil was not going to let go of the rope he was dragging me along by that soon or that easily, no matter how far I journeyed, no matter how hard I tried to rid myself of it.

We set out along the king's highway, skirting the city wall, still silent and deserted. There was no smoke, nor traces of bonfires, nor peasants living nearby, nor cattle, only the stench drifting in the air. No one had returned, and the gloomy, forbidding wall, that awesome silence swept by the wind, was more terrifying there below its gates as it sent back the clatter of the cartwheels than from behind our latticed windows. It was like passing through a life without life, alongside a river deader than dead, frozen, amid barren fields killed by frost. Neither of the two of us spoke, nor did the carter. We merely gazed at those double gates, once so teeming with life, so wide open, so confident, and now deserted, with their two panels shut tight day and night, mayhap awaiting the invisible arrival of the Unforgiving One.

The carter remembered the town in its days of splendor, with its fiestas and its weddings, its patron saint's day when it turned itself upside down, emptying out its best finery and jewels into lively, crowded streets. I had never seen it so, but on the other side of its ashen-colored stones I imagined collations and banquets at which so many victuals were consumed, on which such vast sums of money were expended. I could also see in my mind's eye houses of the gentry, of hidalgos who farmed the land, old families such as ours, without a single Jew or Moor in their lineage, of pure blood and known ancestry. I also imagined the generous widows who were benefactresses of unmarried and orphaned girls, the rich gentlemen, honorable commoners, all living together in peace, some on their rents and revenues, others on income from their office or profession. All of them alike were forced to confront the sickness and the lack of rain, the carter said, and so long as heaven did not decree otherwise, they would continue to be at odds with each other and enemies, for the fear of death and poverty arouse man's worst instincts.

The city now lay behind us, and the convent was no more than a dim blur as the first shadows of dusk fell. Seeing it thus in the distance, it looked like a golden-brown solitary ruin, as deserted as the towering ramparts of the town, and about to fall to pieces. No one could imagine that behind its sun-dried bricks, in the shelter of its willows and its mud walls, a few poor women were waiting, hoping in the name

59

of God that a miserable illusion would turn out to be a true miracle. Looking back at the house now, so shabby and forlorn, at the foot of the mighty wall, it was plain to see how insignificant we were, how more or less right my sister was when she said that only those false wounds would be able to improve our lot. There inside, shut up in our chapter room, in our cloisters and cells, between four walls, it was as though the world did not exist except for the expanse of cultivated ground and the wall that one's eyes could make out from behind the lattticed windows; but outside the walls, looking out over the vast plain, seeing the horizon far off in the distance down the highway, there where it met the sky, this world round about us was enormous, and our house by comparison a miserable speck of dust lost in that silent, golden-brown wasteland. If my sister went on with her plan, if our doctor and our chaplain did not speak out against her, perhaps we would manage to raise it up from that same dust, to lift up our heads, to attract the attention of our benefactors. If not, as I now saw clearly, it would be vanquished, erased from memory, divided, converted like so many others into a stable or a dwelling or a grain storehouse.

Meanwhile the carter drove on, happy and carefree, chatting about one thing and another, sharing none of our concerns, his thoughts not dwelling for an instant on serious matters, his one interest being to get back as soon as possible to his village where his family was waiting for him. He was leaving behind him no pressing obligations. It was plain to see that he was only too willing to banish convent and city from his mind, as he spurred on his drowsy mule that was raising such a cloud of dust on the dry, cracked crust of the path that one would have thought it was a great pack train passing that way. Hearing him burst into song every so often calmed my soul. My mood would have been a joyful one if only I could have rid myself of countless memories, my heart as simple and free from care as that of my lay-sister companion, and not the slave of my love, the victim of my pangs of guilt, unable to forget my sorrows and anxieties.

We finally halted at a convent where they were in the habit of putting up sisters from the order on their rare journeys to the court. They kindly offered us supper and a bed, but before retiring we were obliged to answer so many and such weighty questions that an entire day would not have sufficed to do so; whether the sickness was raging in our community, whether we thought it would spread to theirs, what we regarded as the best remedy, what our chaplain thought—was it a punishment for our sins that would one day be over or was it the end of the world?

I with my scant learning and my sister who was more unschooled still tried to answer in the light of our understanding, which was not much, until drowsiness overcame us. As far as I could see, however, that house was not suffering as severe hardships as ours. Perhaps the fact that it had closer ties to the court and had not yet been abandoned benefited its treasury and its larder, along with the fact that it had been founded by a great lady who at that time was still acting as its generous patroness.

The following day, very early, we went on to the town where the cart was to drop us off. It was a day's journey that brought no news or happening worth mentioning, save for the heat that seemed to set the air afire, turning the elms in the meadows into candlewicks. We stopped to eat at midday not far from an old stone roadside shrine, near a spring that thus far had withstood the rigors of the drought. There in the shade of a clump of willows, the carter brought out his wine and bread along with a chunk of cheese that he cut up in thick slices. My companion and I, after saying our prayers and blessing the bits of cured meat that they had given us in the convent, sat eating them beneath the trees sheltering us from the sun, which at that hour seemed about to finish off the mule and melt all the gear.

The heat did not take away the carter's appetite for lively conversation.

"It's plain to see what the Lord is aiming at," he said good-humoredly, pointing to the roadside shrine in front of us. "He's out to roast us to death like that fellow on the cross."

I didn't understand what he meant and, pretending not to have heard what he said, went on doggedly chewing that tough, dry meat, trying at least to take the edge off my hunger. But the lay sister, more curious than I or more ingenuous, was quite ready to seize upon any excuse to fill such empty hours and asked:

"Who is it you're speaking of, brother? Who is that man that the Lord is trying to roast to death?"

"What!" the carter replied. "Did you never hear tell in your convent of that famous father?"

My companion and I looked at each other without answering, as the carter pointed out to us the four stepping-stones like a flight of stairs.

"It was right here, in this very spot, that they burned him to death. Those stones are a witness, placed there as a warning and to make amends to God."

"What sin was he guilty of?" my companion asked.

"Pure and simple lust, sister. What is usually referred to as solicitation in the act of contrition."

The two of us crossed ourselves, and the man, mayhap spurred on by our distress, went on:

"In order to win over the daughters whose father confessor he was, he was in the habit of telling them that God had granted him a special favor."

"What sort of favor?"

"Ridding him of a man's usual amorous yearnings and passions. Hence he preached that there was no sin in his soliciting what nature itself is in the habit of seeking, but that, quite to the contrary, the union of bodies united men's and women's spirits with God, to His greater honor and glory."

My companion averted her gaze, barely understanding his words, and I for my part, brushing off the dust and the crumbs from my habit, rose to my feet to continue the journey as soon as the carter was ready to do so. But apparently he was in no great hurry to take to the road again. On the contrary, more inclined to finish the wine in his wineskin than to hitch up his animal again, he went on:

"There's not much talk of cases such as this around here, but in the big towns that it's my habit to visit each year without fail, people know more about them than the Holy Tribunal does. There are cities that not even twenty notaries or a hundred inquisitors would be able to clean up, or even take the necessary depositions in. The confessors, the pious church women, and the procuresses in them are all up to so much mischief that they keep them in a constant uproar."

He reluctantly rose to his feet and went to get the mule, being eaten alive by flies.

"That's what happens when so many friars turn into gallant lovers and so many priests into paramours," he concluded.

Night had already fallen when we reached the end of our journey with the carter, a town where we thought we would find lodgings. But perhaps because of the hard times or out of fear of the sickness, the few people still awake at that hour seemed so aloof and unfriendly that we decided to sleep in the open air.

It pleased God to send us a servant, a relative of the carter who had brought us, who gave us shelter in a large house fallen to ruin that he was in the habit of letting out to vendors on market day. And there, with no other light than that of the stars, we slept till midnight, or rather I slept, for the lay sister merely sat in a corner on a pile of straw, staring at the wall as though that friar burned to death at the roadside shrine were about to appear.

At about midnight she awakened me.

"Sister, can what the carter said be true? Can men be such slaves of their bodies?"

It was plain to see that the thought of that perverted confessor haunted her, that her mind was till going round and round even at that late hour, that despite being a lay sister and all, the carter's words had revived long-forgotten fears within her. She looked all about her as though one of those men of whom she was apparently so terrified might be hiding in the shadows. I told her to set her mind at ease, that we were safe there, that she should try to sleep till dawn, for we still had a long way to go before we reached my father's village.

But she persisted.

"Sister, if a man should suddenly appear, what could we two lone women do?"

It was plain to see what a simple-hearted soul this lay sister was.

"Go to sleep," I answered. "And if you can't, when that man that you're talking about comes, wake me up and we'll try to find out what he wants of us. Meanwhile, we had best get some rest if we can, because sleep is a capricious friend and once you reject its advances it may not return and we'll be weary-eyed all day tomorrow."

She heeded my words, lay down alongside me, and didn't get up again until the new day brought from outside the sound of bells ringing.

Soon afterward, two sisters came looking for us, wanting us to come with them to their community. I tried to explain to them that we were obliged to hasten on, but they were so insistent that we finally gave in, on condition that we would stay with them only long enough to take communion and find another means of continuing on our way, which would not be easy since the town was small and not as rich or magnificent as ours, and the lands round about more like peasant farms than ancestral estates.

The convent too was a poor one, its chapel with a roof in such a bad state of repair that the sky was plainly visible from inside, a house so far off the beaten track that it received few alms and so dilapidated that it beggared belief that it was still standing. Those saints who took us to their hearts tried to get us to tarry longer, but when a person is in a hurry, will wins out, and I very much wanted to see my father, though for all I knew he might be already dead and buried by this time.

We stayed only a day with them, answering the usual questions as to the sickness that had left the fields empty, that had put great lords and villeins at odds with each other, that had sowed not only the fear of death but quarrels and dissatisfactions as well, a sad relic of its grievous passage.

Some of the sisters blamed our trials on our sins, others on the Lord's desire to punish us; I for my part maintained that each one of us was suffering for a reason that weighed heavily on our conscience. What weighed most heavily on mine was the memory of my sister's falsehood. What path would she take? Would she have avowed the truth already or would she be going on as I had left her, aloof from the others, remaining silent, lying about her favor in God's eyes, the grace of those fabricated wounds? Was she still thinking of me? Did the memory of me still bring joy to her heart? A cruel torment that: remembering her each night without having her lying beside me, without feeling her side nestling against my side, her skin on my skin, my humble breast on her haughty one, that trembling breath born of the touch of her lips, her devout words, her overwhelmed silences.

Sometimes in my dreams the Lord showed her to me, I could hear her voice, feel her hands in my hands, her mouth, at times rough and at others tender and placid, her paltry crumbs of love I so yearned for.

Or else it was the Devil himself who showed her to me, so good a painter as to compel me to do penance afterward, as though it were not penance enough to miss her so, to feel her so far away, to live my whole life in a half-sleep.

And so, amid my sorrow and my memories, I spent the day and the night alongside my companion who knew no such cares, until, as dawn was breaking, we were able to continue on our way, somewhat consoled and comforted.

Dear Lord, how hard the paths that obedience obliges us to follow! I would be much better off scrubbing the floor of the chapter room, polishing everything in the locutory till it gleamed, or gathering firewood for the kitchen. Better an industrious ant in the house, a perpetual lay sister, than my sister's guardian and companion across the barren plain on her way back home. The dust again blots out everything, the untilled fields and the stumps of grapevines, the wheat that never ripened and the dried-up clusters of grapes. The earth pants like someone gravely ill, the hills bare their flanks blurred with broom the color of ashes. The crown of many a poplar is thin and sparse, as though the water that is its life had not reached its top, and the pines, heretofore always so lovely, are shedding their worm-infested bark and needles. The dead vistas in the distance, the transparent crystal of the rocks, seem motionless, no longer vibrant or glowing as they once were, the new carter tells us. The entire plain that we are crossing neither lives nor breathes; it has dried up, and to my mind it will never again be what it once was, with its abundant streams and its fallow fields turned into a sea of grain and flocks of sheep. Nowadays no one can tell that these wastelands were once paradise, that here the grapes that were gathered and the wheat that was harvested filled many a winepress and many a granary, that that paradise has now turned into a pitiful, mortified purgatory.

Were it not for the crosses that appear along the wayside, an abandoned roadside inn here and there, eaten away by the sun and the wind, it would be very hard to believe what the carter tells us: that this was once a lively road, marked off not by traces of adobe walls but by the warm hearths of those who live by mining coal, by their singing in the distance and their black-faced columns. The land was fertile then and peopled by men of all trades and professions, with a great many

67

deep draw-wells and gardens, with churches and hospitals. Today nothing of all that remains, only dry hard mud and here and there some beast half eaten alive by flies that in this blind world are as much at home as great lords on their feudal estates. Everything round about—sky, fields, streams—proclaims death, leaves us with heavy hearts, and dries up our vitals as well, with no other consolation, no other sound than the monotonous pounding of the mule's hoofs.

But suddenly in a bend in the road there appears a place bright with greenery, full of white flowers so lovely I am at a loss for words to describe them, and in the center of them a figure like an angel or a saint signing to us to tarry there.

The sight leaves me disturbed and breathless, wondering if it is Our Lord or Satan himself come to confound us, but the figure does not move, nor is it discountenanced when we ask it where it is going, what it wants. When the cart halts, it climbs in and the mule, as though obeying an order from it, starts up again, though no one has tugged on the reins.

The four of us continued on in silence; our new carter, who shortly thereafter turned out to be a truck gardener, my companion and I, and behind us the friar, for that was what he was, curled up in a ball inside his ragged, dark-colored habit, thin as a rail and looking as though all his bones were disjointed. His face had lost all its color, his nose hung down so far it almost touched his lips, and his serge habit was in such a sorry state, so oft-patched and threadbare that it barely covered that handful of contorted, ill-smelling bones.

He spoke up finally.

"I would not want to abuse your charity, sisters," he said, "but would you by any chance have a crust of bread you could give me? I've been wandering about the countryside here in these parts for three days now without a single mouthful to eat."

And since none of the three of us answered, he repeated his question once again. Finally my lay sister offered him a handful of figs that he finished off in no time, and the carter a bit of wine that he likewise did not refuse, though it was plain to see that he didn't much care for the taste of it. We did not halt at midday to eat. Time passed quickly as we chatted with our new philosopher-friar who, between requests for yet another sip of wine to assuage his thirst, entertained us with news of the court.

But as the wine disappeared beneath the assaults of the two of them, he dropped the subject of the court and instead began a discussion about the human and the divine. And on this head our gardener proved to be a far more good-humored and discerning man than we had imagined.

"Brother," he murmured, draining the last few swallows in the wineskin, "I'm not one to condemn these and other such pleasant moments in this life."

"Nor am I," the friar answered him.

"Anyone can see that. Even though outwardly you look more like a hermit than a man given to dissipation."

Hearing these words, the friar fell silent, but the carter was not at all inclined to let the conversation lag; on the contrary he was ready and willing to continue the discussion.

"Dissipated or not, you strike me as a man who's not much in favor of abstinences and fasts."

"Neither of fasts nor of any other sort of outward ceremony."

"The Lord be praised!" the other murmured, turning around to look at the two of us. "We have here with us one of those famous Illuminati whose souls are enlightened only by good wine and good meat."

"Both are creatures of the Lord and as such we must accept them."

"That's precisely the sort of creatures I was about to mention," the carter answered, laughing. "That carnal passion that those who belong to that sect say they feel, those leaps and palpitations of the heart that torment them, that aching and exhaustion when a woman is at their side, and by that I don't mean the kind caused by the shaking and jolting of my cart."

"It's quite evident that you have little faith, or little knowledge of the things whereof you speak, which amounts to the same thing. But I should like you to know that many times such effects, and others besides, such as hearing noises and strange voices, are not simply the mercy of the Holy Spirit, and that one of those Illuminati that you hold in such disdain has prepared for the king our sovereign a written report explaining the reasons for this phenomenon."

"It will be a miracle if it ever reaches him."

"Why wouldn't it?"

"What I mean is, without the man's being beaten within an inch of his life."

"I don't believe that a risk such as that will frighten him off," the friar stubbornly insisted. "Many other martyrs were regarded as heretics and sinners during their lifetime only to be received in heaven as saints."

"I can assure you that I too would find such a prospect

pleasing: spending my life here in this world amid devout women, bare naked and in swaddling clothes, and then after my death begin all over again up there in heaven, but at a less tender age and with greater strength."

With a gesture of scorn, the friar hunched down even further in the back of the cart, as though his ribs were insensitive to all that jerking and jolting, and finally murmuring:

"There are many who think that the life of the elect consists solely in taking their pleasure and sinning, but I can tell you that as far as I know there are many among that flock whose life is a living example for one and all."

"That must be so. If not, how to explain that so many men and women seek them out, the former asking for their advice concerning their aches and pains and ailments and the latter touching their rosaries to their persons and tearing off strips of their garments to carry away as relics?"

"It is as you say. They act like bees of Christ gathering the honeydew of their words. I know of a certain one visited by no less than forty coachloads of people a day."

"I'd be quite satisfied with less!" the gardener replied with a sigh. "With the alms of a mere half that number!"

My companion barely turned her face to look at the friar. She merely crossed herself from time to time as she listened to his arguments, and though she gazed off into the distance, trying to make the journey that lay ahead seem shorter, a road still to be traveled that I too found far too long, at times her eyes lighted up beneath the canvas awning and her temples, beaded with sweat, glistened in the semidarkness.

I too knew of that other malady that raged within our religion in those days, worse than any bodily affliction, and I was not at all surprised by that stubborn difference of opin-

71

ion between the friar and the gardener, since even among the most sagacious, most upright, most saintly doctors of theology all discussion of the subject invariably ended up in the same heated argument over the same points. With the carter attacking and the friar defending his position, the final hours of our second journey went by without our noticing. Already, in a break in the barren plain, there huddled my father's village, even more badly stricken by the drought than when I left it, more dilapidated, further reduced to ruins.

The animal pens appeared to be empty, the adobe walls fallen to pieces, the gardens and orchards destroyed, the doors and the windows of the houses yawning open in their cane frames, and the rafters ripped away. It was as though a hurricane had blown through those dirty, black plots of ground, carrying off inhabitants and cattle alike as it passed. Only the sound coming from some enclosure or other, the pounding of an invisible hoe attacking clods of earth as hard as rocks, told us that there was still someone around amid those wretched walls where once everything flourished, at the foot of that church of stone and mortar topped with its Palm Sunday branch of rosemary.

Despite such powerful ill omens, that forbidding silence, the paths so bone dry and so faint as to be barely discernible, my heart leapt as we arrived in front of my house, beyond the empty public square and its dead fountain where in days past so many cattle came to slake their thirst.

I ordered the gardener to halt, and as he sat there absorbed in his discussion with the friar, I entered, with my lay sister following behind, that humble front hallway from which I had left the house years before with a copious flood of tears and promises. No one, not even the family watchdog, came to greet us, and I, knowing the way by heart, soon reached my father's bedside. Though he had not recognized my step, his head was turned toward the door. Seeing him there all by himself, so emaciated, abandoned by one and all, I burst into tears as on the day of my departure when we separated. He must have been aware of very little around him, for he merely looked at me without really seeing me, without muttering a single word, perhaps expecting that someone was bringing him medicine or alms. He lay there, wasted away to skin and bones, with his white beard pointing downward from his jaw and his mind gone, aware of nothing save the sickness gnawing away at his aching body.

Then my own sister, the one who had sent me word, arrived, and shortly thereafter her husband. I learned from them that my father had been laid low for half a year now, with a continual fever, unable to leave his bed.

They did not know whether it was the same sickness that everybody was suffering from, which had hit him harder because he was such an old man, or some particular ailment due to his advanced years, but they had applied blistering cups full of salt, a remedy highly recommended for drawing poisons from the chest, to no avail. He had endured everything with that same serenity with which he had confronted everything his whole life long, until one day he began to be delirious and no longer recognized those who were taking care of him.

I asked them for permission, since my house was now theirs, to stay in it with my companion so that by praying together we might, if not cure him, at least bring him consolation in this difficult moment.

The husband, who appeared to be an upright and reasonable man, raised no objection, and thereupon the truck gardener went back whence he had come and the friar found shelter, as was his habit, in one of the empty barns.

For three weeks we prayed at the foot of my father's bed. Though each morning found me short of sleep, I nonetheless helped out around the house, doing the tasks that always needed doing, or else in the garden, though it required little care now, dry and ruined as it was. The lay sister slept in a corner of the kitchen till it came time to prepare meals.

Thus three weeks passed, until one morning I suddenly missed my lay sister. I thought she must be out in the yard, satisfying bodily needs that one does not speak of, but time went by and she still was not anywhere around. I looked in all the corners of the house, in the garden, and the back yard, but found nothing, not a trace of her, not a sign of her having passed that way.

Outside our walls, the village was silent. Only cicadas and crows were up and about as usual, and the wind was calm, as though fearing to awaken the sun, to sweep the mist away from the plain. I wondered again where my companion could be, and suddenly there came to me in the yard something like a warning, a call from the Lord that illuminated me and led my footsteps beyond the adobe wall around the yard to the barn with the caved-in roof where the friar had taken to sleeping since our arrival. As I drew nearer, my heart began to beat faster, for I had a stronger and stronger premonition that some new misfortune lay in wait for me. I carefully opened the door, and immediately a tense murmur and the sound of sobbing reached my ears. I didn't dare to take a close look, but there, amid the little bit of wheat harvested

74

that year, I saw our philosopher-friar, naked as Adam, on top of my lay sister.

It was his voice murmuring, in softer and even more eloquent tones than on the journey, as tender and honeyed as though born of the flesh itself, and though no words were forthcoming from my lay sister, that infantile and tremorous sobbing, those deep, fervent sighs, were hers.

I withdrew and waited, and in a little while I saw that sinner appear in the door, spreading her skirts, covering her bosom, looking all around before hopping out, tucking back the hair that was now peeking out below her coif. The silence reassured her and finally, without glancing back toward the barn· where her lover and companion remained behind, she slowly walked back toward the house, went inside, and soon was fast asleep, as though her love-adventure had been only a dream.

I for my part closed my eyes in vain. However hard I tried to keep my mind on my father's state, I could not forget that rooting amid the straw, my sister's red face, her tottering footsteps after a moment of pleasure snatched in haste beneath that emaciated man, all arms and legs. Very soon I saw myself in her place, as though in my sister's arms back there in our convent, and the difference was so great that I could not comprehend how women of sensibility, accustomed to warm and tender affection, could choose the rougher and harsher of the two paths offered them, no matter how eloquently men pleaded with them. It was no doubt quite easy to lead my lay sister, a simple, dull-witted companion, to that sheepfold where men have their way with women. Surely those stories recounted in the cart, after her prolonged abstinence in the convent, made her senses reel and caused her to dream of wicked pleasures and delightful raptures. She was still asleep, a sleep like that of animals, like that of those men who, once they have eaten and drunk their fill, gladly and willingly surrender to that little death. Seeing her asleep like that, I felt great scorn for her, and remembering her friar, I wondered what new stories he had whispered in her ear, what new lies he had told her to sway her night after night. But no doubt it had not required any great effort on his part since, as I said before, a woman's will is weak and once she is enslaved by a man, its power declines, her senses are overwhelmed, and her good intentions reduced to nothing.

The scene I had stumbled upon made me sick at heart. I barely spoke to my companion during the next few days, and I had the impression that she for her part deliberately avoided me. She seemed to be more arrogant and defiant than before, and from time to time she took off down the path that I already knew all too well. She even dared to explain to me that since Our Lord had expiated everyone's sins, it was time now to gather His children together, to reap the harvest that those before us had sown for us. Thus nothing was a sin in her eyes. The counsel of that accursed friar was evident in her words, as in her absences that sometimes lasted all night. Her friend had taken possession of her senses and her reason, claiming that whoever made confession to him had earned a place in heaven no matter how heavy the chains of sin and error that he or she dragged about here on this earth.

He had also convinced her that it was useless to invoke the aid of the saints, whereupon she shattered all the images she could lay her hands on. And what was even more of a trial to me, he convinced her that the servants of God should not do any sort of manual labor. Hence she went about drowsily daydreaming all day long, attending to none of the tasks around the house and never giving me a helping hand with mine at my father's bedside, and was wide awake only at night when all the rest of us in the house had fallen asleep exhausted.

But dead tired or not, we went on caring for my father till the Lord saw fit to take him from us. It was wondrous to see how he recovered his powers of reason at the end, giving everyone good final counsel and asking us to forgive him for all the trouble he had caused us. He lived three days more and then suddenly left us one night, as serenely and peacefully as though he were ascending straight to heaven. And when it came time to take him to his final resting place there in the cemetery next to the church, we found my companion missing again. I thought she was with her friend, but there was no sign of the friar either. We didn't see either of them again, and someone from the village told us later, at the supper that we members of the family gave, that he had seen her heading away from the town very early that morning, following in the friar's footsteps along the hillsides covered with olive trees. I was assured that they looked like two pious pilgrims, but knowing them, I had a fair idea where it was that her devotion was taking her, remembering her nights in the barn, her absences, her many follies.

The two of them had taken off, if not in shame at least in secret. My lay sister had not even come to bid me goodbye, perhaps at the urging of the friar, who could well have been afraid that if the two of us found ourselves alone together, she might repent. So they had deserted the Lord, more to follow the way of the flesh than to improve their fortunes in some way. Dear God, how great is Thy goodness toward those who thus crucify Thee a second time; not with nails or thorns, but with their sins, with the blindness of their souls as they follow their earthly appetites!

And I too left my village, in tears once again just as years before, though this time for very different reasons, trying to forget these days surrounded by the sorrows of so many others, with no one to talk to about my own tribulations, at once impatient to return to my convent and fearing that return, since it would bring a meeting with my true sister.

That return took place two days later, at about sext, when no one was expecting me. The entire convent descended like an avalanche upon me. How were things going there outside the walls? How bad was the sickness? What did the harvests promise to be like? What news had I brought back from other communities? One would almost think that I had gone off as an ambassadress to court, rather than back to my village to bury my father in his miserable native soil. I tried to explain that the countryside looked just as it had for some time, with almost no farmhands or cattle, that everyone was awaiting his last hour as once upon a time people waited for hailstorms, that one could scarcely tell the living from the dead. I didn't want to say a word, above all in front of the prioress, about what the carter had told us during the journey, much less recount the love-adventure of our lay sister, and when they asked me about her I lied for charity's sake, assuring them that she too had fallen ill and had stayed behind at her parents' house for a few days until she recovered.

Her life in common with the friar or her tender affection for him, her heresies for which she would surely pay in the end, mattered little to me at that moment. What I wanted most after so many questions, after so many pointless replies, was to know what had happened to my sister, why she was not there with the others. Was she perhaps ill again or being punished?

The first piece of news about her was that while I had been in my village, the chaplain had visited her.

"Well, let us see," he had said to her in his usual paternal tone. "First of all: Do you trust me? Do you believe that I'm here for your own good?"

She had nodded her head in reply and the chaplain had then wanted to know how the wounds in her hands had appeared.

"I've already told you," she had answered. "They must have appeared while I was sleeping. When I awakened, the Lord had imprinted them."

"So you even saw Him?"

"I believe so."

"In your dreams?"

My sister had nodded once more, apparently calm though slightly fatigued, weary of repeating the same explanations over and over again.

"How did you know that it was the Lord? Did you see Him with the eyes of your body?"

My sister seemed not to understand. The chaplain then explained to her that those who maintain that they truly see

God in this life may fall into heresy. She was silent for a moment, as though searching her memory, and then murmured:

"No, not with the eyes of my body."

"With those of the soul then?"

"I don't know. I've already told you that it was in my dreams."

"And how did you know that it was the Lord? Did He speak to you?"

"I didn't hear any words; I didn't feel anything. Only that He was there at my side and was wounding my hands with His fingers till they were like they are now."

The chaplain had had serious doubts, to the point that he had proceeded to consult the prioress as to the health of the ailing sister and her earlier illnesses; then that pertinacious man had insisted on going over the subject yet again with the latter, his manner even more grave than on previous occasions.

More questions and again the same replies, until the chaplain, seeing that discussion was pointless and feeling very weary himself, left off questioning her till a more propitious moment when he would be able to find another way of challenging her story.

As the prioress bade him farewell, the other sisters could see the saint through the door left ajar. According to what they said, she was standing next to the window that overlooked the wall, seeming to be gazing beyond the autumn clouds, to be hearkening to a voice that none of the others heard, to be enraptured by that strange presence that she maintained was ever at her side, plunging her into the immense sea of divinity, leaving within her the memory of His wounds. It was as though the Holy Spirit was at work within her, preparing her for new miracles, though who could say when they would take place or what form they would take?

They saw her thus many times afterwards, motionless, in silent prayer, not seeing or recognizing anyone, making no attempt to appear at choir, much less share the daily tasks of the house.

Her fame and her mortifications, her silence and her decorum, along with the special treatment accorded her by the prioress, were little by little undermining the tranquility of the community, which was now all excited and in a continuous uproar. One afternoon when the sun was hidden behind clouds we saw the sky turn bright red, as though the city were going up in flames. We all contemplated that sudden hellfire wondering if this were the end of time. There were some who prayed for the saint to intercede for us, to raise her voice unto God, to save us. Others, on the contrary, maintained that all that blood staining the horizon was merely a warning that the Lord was sending to our house. A warning of misfortunes yet to come if we persisted in regarding the wounds as evidence of a miracle.

"And why shouldn't it be one?" someone cried. "Isn't this a time of special graces and miracles? A scourged Infant Jesus appeared in Toledo; he too was dripping blood. There are many people who swear to it."

"And in the convent of Los Ángeles, a sister who went up to the rooftop terrace to hang out clothes saw a star in the sky, blinding-bright. And that very same month her soul passed on to the Lord."

We all remained there in silence, gazing beyond the latticed windows at the crimson sky, its color softer now at its edges tinged with gold. None of the sisters could bring herself to leave or to pray. All of us simply stood there, hoping that the Lord would call us to His presence too, all of us a prey to a vast anxiety in the face of that threat for which each of us had her own explanation.

"They say that there have been earthquakes in Burgos."

"And hunger and drought as well—the same as here."

"And they say that in Flanders soldiers saw two armies fighting in the sky."

"And a bottomless well has appeared in La Mancha all of a sudden."

"And a river of turquoises in Zamora."

"Can that be true?"

"Why not? Aren't there other rivers that have gold in them? I myself saw one when I was a little girl."

We all stood there next to the latticed window, trembling, not daring to peek out, with the eyes of our bodies fixed on the others and the eyes of our souls tightly closed to shut out the light of our senses. We could already see ourselves before the Lord, accounting for our sins—myself above all, being in large part responsible for this entire fabrication, for all this pretense and all these flights of imagination, for the growing fame of my sister, who was already beginning to be looked upon as a saint.

It was time, then, to call things by their rightful name, to break the pact between us and bring out into the light of day the truth of those hands which, on an ill-starred night, I had pierced out of love and out of love had claimed were evidence of a true miracle, with their two wounds that were the color of roses at the time and now—so they said—were all black and still gaping open.

I knocked at her door and no one answered. I knocked again and the door opened little by little, leaving us suddenly face to face. My sister, taken by surprise, pretended not to see me, and very slowly, as though stealing away, walked back across her cell and seated herself on her bed. I crossed the threshold, murmuring in a soft voice:

"Your Charity may raise her eyes. It is I, truly here, in person."

"So you've finally come back."

"Yes, here I am, ready to listen to your arguments. When are we going to tell the truth?"

My sister sighed and asked in turn:

"What truth? We haven't even begun yet. Are you still afraid?"

I silently nodded my head. The truth was that I was trembling all over, finding myself so close to her after so long a time.

"It frightens me to deceive the sisters, to hear them talking the whole day long of miracles."

"Why listen to them then? In any event, before a year has passed it will all be over and done with."

"A whole year still?"

And she, in her calm voice that sounded as though it were

coming from a long way away, not from the lips of the sister who had been my friend, answered:

"What does a mere year matter? Very little, if our goal is the salvation of this house."

"Don't count on me to keep silent that long. I shall not be able to."

"Yes, you will. If only by dint of keeping your mind fixed on that other life that awaits us afterward."

I sat down beside her, my hands in hers as in times past, my head on her breast, saying not a word, trembling. From outside there came a sudden warm wind that seemed to envelop me from head to foot, to pass through me, to fill my eyes with tears and bring beads of sweat to my forehead, but this time my sister seemed to be oblivious to me, hard of heart and hostile to my tenderness. Seeing her so detached, so different, so unresponding, I murmured, seeking refuge in her lap:

"Ever since the day we committed our grave misdeed, I can find no consolation. It is time now that I find peace once more with you."

And the remedy was even crueler than my suffering, for her hands rose to my face and for the first time I was able to have a close look at them. They were the very image of our sin, as if the Malign One who seeks our perdition had buried his claws in them and torn away the flesh. Like the cancer that eats away women's breasts, unleashing its poison to the very dregs, so there welled forth secret humors beneath that skin, once as delicate and soft as the caress of angels. It was plain to see that our sin was destroying that flesh, so acutely painful now.

"In God's name, I beg you not to touch me."

And my sister, contemplating her wounds, asked me in an offended, surprised voice:

"What! Does shame at what you have done so readily overcome you?"

Out of pity I refused to answer her, but she immediately understood my revulsion and hid them from sight again, barely listening to me when I said to her:

"The two of us will end up in hell, thanks to you."

"You are quite right: the two of us, together. In hell or in heaven; no one will ever be able to separate us now. What more do you want?"

My constant fear abandoned me yet again. Once again my soul was hers, my body, my salvation, my will entirely hers. The two of us were together once more beneath our rough serge habits, atop that burlap bedcover so often darned and mended, our past miseries again shared, consoled, friends once more, our hair and our coifs tangled together, sighs and sobs in the dead-quiet cell, far from our sleeping sisters, from the tranquil silence of the afternoon siesta. Chastisement or death concerned us not at all. No punishment, however rigorous, would be capable of breaking that sweet, strong embrace, of effacing the memory of that new, eager pleasure.

Suddenly we heard a dull rumbling above our heads. We lay there in suspense, both of us overcome with fear and trembling, as though it were the voice of God sending down his worst curse upon our heads, as though threatening to annihilate us. Then the sound was repeated, breaking above terraces and rooftops, and again farther away, rolling across the entire plain beyond the walls, driving the frightened birds from the cloister. Suddenly the countryside seemed changed, alive, threatened. Gusts of wind raised heavy dust whirls, gathering and swirling across the open fields, pursuing each other up into the sky, dark now and filled with flashes of lightning. They followed one upon the other, ripping the belly of the clouds apart, chasing each other, destroying each other, fleeing at times only to return to the attack, stubborn and powerful, leaving the house stunned.

Suddenly a light brighter than a thousand suns tore the sky apart and we saw, there in infinity, a great golden throne. There was no one seated upon it, it appeared to be empty, and yet the two of us were paralyzed with fear. Someone far above was gazing down upon us and judging us, someone whose hand seemed to me to be threatening us. His voice was the sound of the hard constant wind blowing, his hand was like a cloud that changes shape almost the moment one sees it, so that like mist rising from the earth one can retain no memory of it.

Our courage, that inner fire, was little by little abandoning us; our souls no longer animated our bodies which, for lack of that inner heat, were carried away by that incandescent light. And so we lay in each other's arms, oblivious to everything that was not light and love round about us until the sound of rain lashing the earth brought us to our senses once again.

It was raining at last, the odor of garden and field, long since disappeared and forgotten, returned, that fresh smell that swept away the dust in the fields covered with dry stubble, turned now into a dirty, raging torrent. Voices and hymns rang through the cloisters, praying to God that the rain would not cease to fall.

The joyous drumming of the great drops on roof tiles and gutters foretold better times once again, and in answer to our prayers the Lord blessed us with rain from heaven for so many days on end that the reservoir was filled to overflowing and the fields, clean and glistening, were left ready for grain to be sowed.

Chapter Three

THE rain that washed away the dust now turned to mud along the paths and in the garden beds took with it the sickness as well, as it had at other times. Little by little the health of those sisters who were ill improved. It was a pleasure to hear the sound of water pouring down from the sky, blotting out the walls, soaking deep into the earth, restoring the dark luster of the blackberry vines and the color of the fruit trees in the orchard.

Day by day the convent came back to life. Dawn found all of us once again up and about reciting our first prayers; it was the witness of our meditations and our reading in the hours before mass brought us together in the chapel again, shivering with the cold but healthy and happy. And the moment the bell rang to tell us that noon had come, we fell to our knees for the daily examination of our consciences.

I always found nothing for which to reproach myself, save for the matter of the wounds, for I never regarded it as a sin to love the Holy Creator by loving His humble creatures, nor did I look upon myself, His meek servant, as being capable of failing to do His will in any way, as do Turks and heretics and that friar who had spread his net to trap my poor lay sister. Once we have delivered our free will into the Lord's hands, how can we resist temptations? In perpetual prayer, how can we possibly offend Him, when the love shared by His creatures is more sacred than all other virtues? As my sister assured me, perfect souls have no reason to fear that they will find themselves before the tribunal of penitence, since God multiplies the effects of the Sacrament, granting them His grace forevermore.

Hence when it came time for confession, she lied. I too lied, the two of us now one, body and soul, the whole day through, so much so that the prioress, guided—who knows?—either by her own keenmindedness or by words of warning from another, finally caught us out one day when we were together, on the bank of the reservoir, at the afternoon siesta hour.

She summoned us before her; she reminded us that always keeping the same company was against the rules of the house, and threatened to punish us if we did not mend our ways, after having been duly warned this first time.

I was well aware of the rules, I knew full well that no sister was to have any one particular friend, since each of us was the sister and friend of all, nor were we to touch the face of another, much less go so far as to kiss it, but above all else I saw in our superior's warning a sign of ill-will toward my sister that with time was beginning to reveal itself. For insofar as discipline was concerned, we were far less lax than the rest of the community. Our heads never nodded in the choir like those of so many of the sisters, whose excuse was that they were sleepy, nor did we spit on the stairs and then erase with our foot such a trace of bodily filth, as did a number of them. On the contrary, my sister and I—she despite her bandaged hands—spun, embroidered bridal gowns sent us from the city now that weddings were being held once again. It is quite true that at times we murmured a few words, but who among the sisters was completely faithful to her vow of silence? Only the oldest ones, who had lost all desire to know what was happening in the world of the living, whether or not the noble lords of the town had returned from the court yet or only those who farmed the land, ever eager not to miss out on the coming harvest.

That was not the reason for the change that had come over the prioress, in the old days the mother of all the sisters and now, ever since the matter of the wounds, suddenly become their judge. She put an end to chats together at night, though this did not put an end to our sleepless nights. On the contrary, the sisters continued to be unruly and quarrelsome, to the point that two novices came to blows over a choir-stall.

The two were immediately punished by being confined to their cells for an entire week. It was quite something to see how much plotting it took, how many difficulties had to be surmounted to get to see them and cheer them up a bit, how much ingenuity was required merely to smuggle a little fruit from the orchard in to them.

Disorder and pettiness reigned in the house, until finally matters came to a head in exactly the way we had imagined they would. It happened on a certain night when, as usual, my sister came to visit me. It may be that it was a punishment from God, or love, that stopped the ears of both of us. In any event, the door was suddenly flung wide open, as though by a gust of wind, and we saw the prioress appear on the threshold with her lamp in her hand. We did not have time to slip out of each other's arms. She stood there looking at us with those weary, listless eyes of hers suddenly blazing with anger, like flashes of lightning in the darkness. Her words fell upon us one by one, concise, grave, threatening our bodies, staining our souls, not so much wounding us as humiliating us.

As usual I began to tremble, far from those arms that a moment before had been protecting me, but my sister, who suddenly seemed to be another person altogether, began to threaten her enemy in turn, as though she were not at all afraid of her. Her anger made the prioress reel, for my sister threw into her face her neglect of the convent, her bad management of its alms and its property, her indolence in collecting tithes in the days when they were still to be had, the debts that had been contracted, the lands and bequests that had been lost, her abuse of power on this or that occasion.

The prioress heard her out without uttering a word in her own defense. When my sister had finished, all she said was that that was not the proper place for such arguments.

"I stand by every word that I have said," my sister answered. "I am ready to repeat all of it before the entire community."

But the prioress did not appear to be willing to allow this, and a few days later, my sister, with her back bared, paid for her sin and mine, in accordance with the established rules of the order.

There she was, lying face downward on the tile floor of the refectory, wounded twice over, her hands first and now her pride, before the eyes of the whole community, before my eyes bathed in tears. Where, I asked myself, was that oft-proclaimed love of all sisters for one another, as Christ commands? Where was forgiveness, the refusal to take vengeance? Perhaps it was simply yet another test, a way of pointing a finger at us, above and beyond our deception, of erasing whatever sin lay behind that false miracle. Perhaps Our Lord wished to efface those wounds by means of these new ones, at once cruel and genuine, inflicted by our enemy whose stubborn wrath had caused her to take leave of her reason. Then as the leather strap fell again and again upon those soft shoulders, so welcoming in days gone by, I was not the only one to burst into tears, for others near me began to weep as well at the sight of that impassive face that seemed to be stoically counting each blow.

But as the sisters lifted the saint up off the floor, it was suddenly quite clear that the path our superior had taken was the wrong one. That was the way we all saw it, and her error was soon evident from the silence with which we obeyed, from the care with which we carried our sister, from the way in which, as if by chance, the others spat on the floor just inside the doorway as they left the refectory.

Our judge remained there all by herself, on her knees, murmuring her prayer alone, begging for a forgiveness that was not to be forthcoming in this life here below.

That angry red back with the broken flesh was slowly healing—with salt water, my love, and my care. Little by little it took on its normal color once again, the humiliating welts disappeared, the down began to grow out again like a soft golden fleece. Despite the pain, the sharp sting of the salt water in the wounds, I never heard a complaint escape my sister's lips, nor did I once feel her body tremble. Though the salt water made the cracks in my fingers burn, it did not seem to hurt her, nor the ointments and pomades that came later, nor the cold of the cell now that autumn was coming to an end.

In my eagerness to see that flesh mended, I was also suffering from something else. If my own flesh could have repaired the damage to hers that the punishment had caused, I would gladly have offered it to her, simply to alleviate in some way the pain of that body that after each treatment I took in my arms and kissed, and then laid back down on the fresh, smoothed straw of the mattress that I had made ready.

As my lips traveled along those paths, once blue but now red, withered, pitiful to see, as my hands sought hers in the cold hollow of her throat, as they met mine, pressed them, fought them until they fell back defenseless into the dark valley between her breasts, my sister came to life once again, if only for a brief time. Then, at that hour, as the two of us waged our love-battle amid pain and pleasure, forgetting the prioress and the entire house, nothing came to trouble our minds, neither past days nor the uncertain future, nor even those wounds through which the sickness within came to the surface of her skin, stubborn, impatient, responding to no treatment, intractable to the advice of doctors. At that hour her open hands were chalices into which to sink my lips as did Our Lord in the vinegar and gall, red-hot embers of our solitary love. Beyond the cell, where the only sounds to reach our ears were the discordant cries of squabbling birds and the monotonous song of the water, nothing existed, no one was listening, no one was watching, no one was awake; there

94

were only the two of us alone at the edge of that flowing spring of her wounds, waiting for nightfall in our paradise, till the first stars began to gleam above the wall.

We were openly at war with the prioress now, and neither her dire threats nor the disapproving gaze of the others mattered to us; fortune was on our side as the appointed day for the new election approached.

What did her hard words, her veiled slights imply? What could she add that we did not already know? All the pleasure of the world was contained within a single moment, not in countless words devoid of all love, empty and dry. Had she ever known such overflowing joys as ours? Old and withered for as long as we had known her, she had never been able to understand our secret, the one that is born alongside the heart that has been struck a dark blow that both mends and rends the painful body. Her enmity toward us seemed like the madness of a virago, of a scorned, resentful, vanquished male. Like all her punishments, it was merely a form of vengeance whose motive was fear, as though in and through our love her dried-up, aged body, never sought after, were feeling all the pain of its years of loneliness and tedium.

The youngest ones must have thought the same thing, for once the sickness fled, bringing a breath of life from outside the convent walls once again, they began to look upon us once more as sisters sharing joys and sorrows, offering us their votes in favor of our cause and against the old days of sadness and submission.

My sister and I responded in like manner; these and other sisters whose minds were not yet made up were won over to our side thanks to that punishment and others even more severe that followed. We convinced so many of her extraordinary virtues that very soon the saint's fame spread to the city.

Hence one day, almost at daybreak, a shadow began prowling about on the other side of the turning-box at the entrance. The portress tried to drive the person away, but then, thinking that it was some farmer who was coming to bring us provisions as in days gone by, she asked:

"What may I do for you, brother?"

"Ave Maria," a female voice answered, for the shadow was a woman. "I've come to ask for something."

"And what is that?"

"That an illness be cured."

"According to what I've heard, the doctor has come back to the city. Go to him, sister, you whom I took for a man a moment ago. He will surely find a remedy for your illness."

"The thing is, I'm not asking for myself," the woman replied, raising the mantle she was wearing, revealing a bundle of modest proportions next to her breast. "I'm asking, rather, on behalf of this baby who neither eats nor sleeps and has a bad fever night and day and an illness from the drought that seems to be causing him to waste away inside."

The portress answered that she would inform the prioress so that all of us might remember the baby in our prayers, but the mother did not give up easily. She began insisting that only the saint's hands could cure the child.

That was the way we first learned of the fame that my sister was gradually gaining beyond our walls in the city, where people were more than willing to believe that those hands whose touch the woman was seeking for her child had brought rain down from the clouds and driven away the latest pestilence.

At such news the prioress grew even more enraged. She barely spoke to us, and the two of us paid her back in the same coin, counting on the fact that time was working in our favor. The Lord willing, the baby was well again in a few days—who can say whether its recovery was due to chance or to devotion? At any event the mother, her faith in the saint grown stronger still, loudly sang the praises of the one who had brought such a thing to pass. And from that time on there was not a day when we were not visited by people of all sorts, humble folk above all, possessed of great fervor and in numbers such that they sometimes filled the portico from the entrance to the turning-box.

The Mother Superior's orders were to no avail, nor were the efforts of the portress to maintain silence among them, to try to satisfy them any more successful. In the beginning we all thought that good times had at last returned after so many afflictions, those days of gifts and offerings when the house, rich in vineyards and land, knew only abundance and material well-being. But we soon saw that we were mistaken. That horde that grew larger and larger came to us with empty hands. It was not the convent that brought them there, but simply the presence of my sister and her hands capable of curing sicknesses, driving away the plague, or saving the harvests. It was only to see those hands, touch them, kiss them, that they were there, each one with his burden of cares, some with one last hope in their eyes; and then there were others, come from farther away, with the signs of some terrible malady, with their air of wretched misery, besieging the turning-box with their pain and their complaints. They had not come to give but to take away; their mood was not a humble and submissive one as in the past, but rather one that turned more

97

surly and disagreeable each time that the prioress closed the doors on them. Hence what at first had been devotion began little by little to turn to wrath, until one day it exploded in the chapel.

One morning, as mass ended, we saw them suddenly turn round, having perhaps agreed among themselves beforehand to do so, and as the bell rang, they walked over to the grating that closed off the part of the chapel reserved for the cloistered sisters. Despite the thick close-set bars, my sister and I managed to make out those pitiful, emaciated faces, openly rebellious now.

"Is the little mother there? Let her approach, we pray you, Your Graces."

"Just her hands, so that we may touch them."

"May she cure these tertian fevers."

"Commend us to the Lord. Save this miserable people."

The prioress tried in vain to convince them that my sister was not among our number. Some of those in the crowd hoisted their children up onto their shoulders, others turned their blind eyes upward, fingering the bars with firm faith, groping for a handhold as they awaited her miraculous presence.

"She is not here," the prioress cried. "The provincial has sent for her."

"That's not true," they answered. "She's been punished and is being kept in her cell. The Lord will not forgive such a thing."

My sister and the entire community remained silent, witnesses of this divine judgment, curious to see how it would end. Suddenly a voice rose above all the others.

"I saw her in the garden this very morning."

And like an echo her companions took up the hue and cry, more tenacious, clamorous, and impassioned still.

"We beg Your Mercy to allow her to return."

"That is impossible, I tell you. Come, come, enough of this! Otherwise we'll close the chapel to visitors once and for all!"

The prioress made a move to draw the curtain covering the grating but managed to close it only halfway. Little by little we saw an avalanche of hands appear between the bars, like those of the damned struggling to escape from hell, and fall upon the panels of the curtain, about to rip them to shreds. That hostile breath, that threatening murmur was drowned out by a dull roar of protesting voices.

"Have all of you forgotten the days when this house lived on our alms?"

"They didn't draw the curtain in our faces then."

"Is this what's meant by charity, sisters?"

"Who was it that drove the sickness away?"

"Who was it that made rain fall?"

"They say she neither eats nor drinks. That the only nourishment she takes is the communion wafer."

"That she has a covenant with Our Lord."

"That the Virgin Mary is ever with her."

Though the voices did not calm down, neither did the prioress give in. She was hoping that the fire would burn itself out, and as the cries gradually died down, she ordered the curtain to be drawn all the way, and abruptly closed the door. When the church was completely empty, after dismissing us with a gesture, she remained there alone, on her knees as usual. She appeared to be imploring the help of the Lord, and seeing her there motionless, so haughty and unbending despite her years, I wondered whether she had not guessed the truth, to what lengths her ill-will toward us would go and how difficult the moment would be that surely lay in store for us, at least insofar as I was concerned, that moment when we would be forced to confess the truth, a confrontation which, as time went by, seemed to me to be more and more inevitable and greatly to be feared.

Winter came at last. It returned with a vengeance this time, in a fury, prepared to get the better of the drought in hand-to-hand combat, to judge from the torrential rains it brought with it. The springs overflowed, the swollen streams pouring down from the mountains flooded their banks and filled the roads with noisily rushing water, sweeping away with it brushwood and adobe walls, mosses and crossweed. The wind, turning warm as night fell, drove before it black armies of lowering clouds that collided with each other like round flint stones, illuminating the sky with sudden flashes as bright as altar lights in the dark. It was another judgment day, not a bone-dry, silent one like the one before, but rather a dark, rumbling one, a battlefield, echoing with the sound of drums and tambours. The birds sought what poor shelter they could in eaves and under rooftops; we could see them shaking the water from their feathers, seeking refuge far from their nests. The sisters contemplated the very entrails of the sky, the rare streaks of light that came from on high and died away above the plain. They too were hoping for something. Not good health or harvests, but some greater grace that would save the house from the ruin that was even more evident now, with roofs gaping open and flooded cloisters. Our little world of broken roof tiles and crumbling adobe walls resounded, sighed, sobbed, in time to the drumming of the rain as the drops kept falling, relentlessly washing away, wearing away, destroying enclosures and walls, leaving laths and plaster exposed, swelling the walls covered with damp stains, leaving them bloated. Though it did not snow, a chill, cruel, unpleasant wind kept blowing, punishing us at every hour of the day, especially at that appointed for prayer and meditation.

Here, all by myself, my soul in its need keeps asking: where is she? Remembering her is grave torment that so whets my desire that, were it not for the eternal hope of being reunited with her, I would take leave of my senses and even of my reason, forgetting entirely where it is that I spend my days. A cruel martyrdom this, that permits me to think only of her, that drives from my mind all concern for, all friendship for the others in this house, even though they too are sisters, friends, companions.

Amid such suffering, in such a state, my heart does not understand; its one desire is to go to her, to be one with her again, body and soul, casting aside fears and rejections.

If only I could be at her side again now, as this rain beats down and washes everything away, in these days when my soul is lost in dreams: the two of us together again, so perfectly one we yearn to die! Her image in my mind, the memory of her, her voice that at times echoes through the cloister, chatting, conversing with the others, leaves my throat dry, my knees weak, my hands so numb that it is impossible to join them now on my poor chastised body.

At times I think that if her fame spreads and people keep

coming despite the rain and their labors, our plot will soon be revealed by words that her own mouth will utter, its threads will come undone, it will come to an end, heaven only knows how, but it will be finished forever. At the moment it is proceeding nicely. It is true that with the roads closed to pack animals and carts, only people on foot come to see the saint, who rarely appears. She is no doubt reserving her favor for better pilgrims, for rich peasants, landowners, and noblemen, but when I think that along with them, as soon as the weather clears, our provincial may also arrive, I await such a crucial moment with mortal fear.

I might do well to forget her, to erase from my heart the memory of this love that prevents me from keeping vigil at night, from sleeping, from reciting my prayers. If I could turn my mind once again to loving the other sisters, I might find myself in better spirits. Virtue, affection, will, and determination invite me to draw closer to them, but if I compare their hands to those mortified hands, their flesh to that other flesh battered and bruised by the cruel embrace of relentless scourges, my heart hesitates no longer and immediately takes her side.

And so I remain floating in the air, deeply concerned about her uncertain future, fearful, racked with sobs. What will we do if people keep flocking to our door, to the locutory, to the chapel? Where will it all end? Now, in this month of December, thanks to the respite that the cold has brought, we can still remain silent, hold people off with pious lies, but when February again brings mild days, the rumors will fly and the crowds that come will be bigger and bigger. What to do then? What to say to the Visitor when he comes? Like spring-fed streams that begin as a mere trickle amid flat river stones but soon flood whole gardens and valleys, pouring over the tops of the adobe walls, so it is with our plot as time goes by. It is flourishing, prospering, unfolding, and it will surely be our undoing if we do not put ourselves out of harm's way very soon. Or perhaps it is not really a plot, not really a deception. It may be that those planned wounds, that deliberate mortification of the flesh are now true wounds as my sister maintains, born in a dream, signs from the Lord, for it is in a dream that we all live and prosper.

During the interminable nights of this winter, such a wet one and such a change after so long a drought, this long overdue rain at once lashes us and laments, filling the chapter room with voices, making us hear the footsteps of the Devil in the distance, who must be going about reaping his harvest as usual. He can be heard snorting, running, tracking down everything that lives or flees him, there just outside the walls, or farther off, in the fields, amid the poplars. A hard and wretched life, this. There is no certain happiness nor any thing that does not change, nor any truth on which to rest one's soul, save for the love that hounds and harasses me day after day.

That night it seemed to me that the Devil or the wind drove me to her cell once more, made me wrap my cape about me as always in winter, and took me along the usual path through the passageways. I was not as happy and breathless with anticipation as on other occasions. My sister's indifference, her way of staring blankly into space, her manner of speaking, colder and more aloof now, her failure to seek me out as she once had, were driving the barb of abandonment deeper and deeper into my very soul, piercing it through and through.

It was a sweet thorn, though bitter at times. In the choir, my wound exuded melancholy. There in her stall next to the choir desk, her expression so serious and grave, whereas the others sat drowsily murmuring psalms, their heads nodding the while, in my eyes she looked entirely different from the rest of us: seated on a throne, chosen by the finger of the Lord, far above our flock, defiant yet still obeying the prioress's voice.

If those who fought so desperately to see her in the chapel could have seen her then, they would have given their life for her, just as I myself would have, they would have flung themselves at her feet, just as I wished to do at that very moment. As I made my way toward her cell in the darkness, the wind uprooted the last crossweeds growing in the walls, bringing bits of plaster and pieces of roof tile dangerously crashing down. The clouds were galloping by, sweeping the turrets of the galleries, the empty eyes of the dilapidated belfry, setting its deep-voiced bronze bell to ringing. It was a bold, insolent wind, as though the Tempter himself were searching about with his hands, arms, and legs amid the folds of my habit.

Suddenly, there in one corner, amid the honeysuckle vines numb with cold, I spied a white cape flying along; I followed it and little by little, step by step, others came to meet her, hugging the walls and pillars for shelter, as far away as possible from those gusts of wind lashing the arches. They were all fighting against the wind, fearing heaven only knew what dangers, mumbling heaven only knows what secrets under their breath.

They cleft the darkness, the shadows of the cloister like a flock of doves, spurred on by an eager desire that I could not divine, but that I suspected was not unlike my own. Hence I followed in their footsteps, fighting against the same wind, trying to overhear a few vague words of explanation, wondering what the reason was behind this secret conclave, until I gradually realized what it was that was being discussed.

As I listened, as phrases, words, echoes reached my ears, it was borne in on me more clearly that the clandestine meeting toward which we were making our way so silently must have something to do with the removal from office of our Mother Superior, who up until then had ruled over our destinies in the house.

That was the reason why she forbade us to chat together, to meet each other at siesta time, to talk together when we were working, to read in secret, or leave our cells before matins. That was the time for reflection, she would say to us, for union with God Who would shed His light on the path to follow in order to come to a fairer decision on the day we cast our votes.

It was not fitting or proper for the oldest sisters to influence the younger ones. The good of the convent must come before our own good, before petty benefits, and therefore we were to elect the sister who would head our house in days to come with no other counselor than our own good sense and reason.

I now clearly discerned that this and no other was the cause of that wandering through the night, amid distant claps of thunder and flashes of lightning. This became more evident still when, a few moments later, those who were ahead of us halted before one of the doors, looking all about like alert sentinels. Their secretive glances must have reassured them, for almost immediately they tapped lightly on the door.

It opened without a sound, as silent as our footsteps. Inside, by the feeble oil lamp that left the corners in deep shadow, I managed to make out so many faces that it seemed as though the community had multiplied. From the very oldest sisters to novices we scarcely knew, crowded together elbow to elbow, squeezed together, pressed one against the other, the entire order seemed to be gathered together there for this Judgment Day, in such numbers that they hid the walls, the window, the little carpet, the door.

Finding myself there among them, not really one of them, a stranger and an outsider, as I observed the others closely I suddenly was seized with grave fear. Having come there by chance without having been invited, the object all of a sudden of so many eyes, gestures, and silence, I sorely missed once more that sister who always lent me life and strength at such crucial moments.

But no one said a word; those who were staring at me forgot my presence almost immediately, and as though thoroughly familiar with the principal matter at hand, returned to their thoughtful considerations, their quiet whispers. Oblivious to the windstorm and the flashes of lightning, they talked together, discussed the subject, tried to arrive at a sort of agreement aimed at ensuring that my sister would be chosen as the new prioress when the election that was rapidly approaching was held. One after the other, the sisters brought to light there in that dark tribunal her virtues and merits, her vocation, her charities, and finally the grace granted her by Our Lord God in the last few months.

And once more I said nothing; the Devil sealed my lips, whispering in my ears words of love, phrases, memories of the saint, calling to mind those benefits she used to speak to me of each day. To my sorrow, I sinned by remaining silent, assenting, agreeing to be a party to a plan with most serious consequences, in which I was already deeply involved.

When in the end, almost without discussion, that dark dovecote of white capes and black wool habits emptied into the dense silence of the night, I was among the last to leave the cell. Again my heart was pounding, again my conscience accused me, but the Devil whispering his evil counsel in my ears, perhaps to damn both my sister and me, made me keep silent once more, to continue on my way with the others, at an uncertain, forlorn hour when dawn was already raising the curtain of clouds above the cracked walls of the garden and the irrigation ditch.

It came time for the election, at once so greatly feared and so eagerly desired. One after the other we took our seats in the chapter room, awaiting the prioress's sermon. Behind us lay entire days of maneuvering for votes, pacts, arguments. Two sisters even came to blows over whether or not the saint was worthy of ruling the house, and whether or not the old prioress was the prime cause of our wretchedness now, of the badly deteriorated and seriously damaged state of our patrimony. One of the two claimed that the prioress's advanced years and the illnesses she had suffered had made her arrogant and lazy, that she often forgot to levy the tithes on the farms and pasture lands belonging to us, and hence they were lost through her negligence.

Her sacristans, that is to say her friends and advocates, counterattacked by accusing the saint of being a fraud and a worker of false miracles, but they did so to no avail, for the majority of the younger sisters were on her side.

Such arguments were the cause of hard slaps. One of my sister's most fervent partisans ended up with a bleeding mouth because of such accusations, while the oldest sisters confessed that they had never before been witness to such rancors and unruliness in the house. But the sister, her lips bloody and her eyes blazing with anger, had gotten up from the floor and like someone who has been well rehearsed, answered heatedly that the prioress, whoever she might be, was obliged to render an accounting to the community every year, something that had never once taken place since the day long ago when this one had been elected.

Her broken voice, overstrained from arguing so long and so hard, was soon joined by others raised in a rosary of protests: that the prioress had sold lands belonging to the community, advanced sums of money for work that was never done, made decisions that disturbed the peace of the house. They pounced like a flock of white crows on that woman who, though admittedly old and all the rest of it, was no doubt not as bad a mother superior as her daughters so loudly proclaimed. Her secret niggardliness and pettiness, her least little faults were uncovered, studied like the vitals of a sick man, exposed to the blinding light of day, from the most recent ones to the most remote, so far back in the past that they had long since been forgotten.

They even dug up an old quarrel about the Christmas Day when she had authorized a few little dances to honor the birth of Jesus, arranged for beforehand with a company of actors who, dressed as kings and accompanying themselves on lutes and guitars, came with some people from the city to bring us a little cheer on a day marked by the Lord as one for rejoicing. Times were more favorable then; the convent was rich, better equipped, with a larger flock. The prioress was an old, old woman now and the incident dated back to her very first years as head of the convent; even so, her enemies did not appear inclined to forgive her for it. The Devil, they said, is the father of all dances and the flesh their mother. Between the two they try to drag mortals down to hell by means of them, and for that reason they were always forbidden in the community, above all in the presence of laymen.

Hearing them, I wondered what special virtue enabled my sister, so distant and grave and silent, with no good reason in her favor, to thus win the others over. What secret strength those hands that I had crippled possessed, capable of unleashing such secret grievances before the voting began! Apart from myself, I had no doubt that there were only two persons in the house who were certain that they knew the truth, each of them in her own way: those two who, sitting on either side of the table where the votes would be counted, were apparently not even looking at each other, ignoring each other, yet beneath their seeming disdain, each of them was pitting against the other a hidden will to power.

The first of the two to arrive had been the prioress, accompanied by four or five of her faithful and the sister she most trusted, the one who assisted her and gave her a helping hand when her strength failed her. Despite her years and the grave events of the last few months, the prioress's step was proud and steady, and even though she leaned on her black cane as usual, she seemed little disposed to abandon her office and authority, her serious infirmities and the new rancor of her charges notwithstanding. She made her way to her stall without help, and setting aside the silver-handled cane she knelt, praying heaven above to enlighten the minds and hearts of all on such a momentous occasion. On hearing those prayers, on seeing her so submissive, fallen to her knees in the dust on the floor, some of us sisters present pondered whether it might not be a despicable decision to remove her from her office, to relegate her for her few remaining years to the lowly status shared by other sisters her age, to the dark corner where useless things lie forgotten. Seeing her there, at our feet so to speak, her face invisible, covered by her coif and her hands, it seemed as though she was asking—not for herself, but for the community, for all her sisters, whether friends or enemies—that the peace of the house not be shattered, that she be allowed to keep her office for a few years more, perhaps until the hour of her death.

And at the same time I asked myself whether all that piety was sincere, whether her prayers were not born of her pride, whether they would really be capable of erasing in the minds of all the other sisters the memory of all her carelessness and neglect, all her niggardliness, obliging them to live like beggars, so to speak, sending off those who were able to do so, for instance, to eat at the homes of their relatives in the city.

In a moment she rose from her knees and remained seated in her stall praying, the beads of her black rosary slipping one by one between her fingers deformed by the dampness, devotions, and the years. A faint, intermittent sound: her voice muttering her barely audible prayer, for her lips scarcely moved; an impatient voice, perhaps one of contained wrath as her rival delayed her appearance and all eyes were turned in the semidarkness toward the half-open door.

Suddenly the prioress's voice fell silent; her rosary lay motionless and the attention of all the sisters was focused on the threshold of the door, where other footsteps, other murmuring voices now broke the stillness.

Shadows darkened the doorway, and one after the other, those who were missing filed in, like a humble and silent cortege, a faithful flock quite different from the one that I had witnessed on previous nights. Enveloped, sheltered in their capes, no one would have guessed that only a short time before they had confronted those present so violently; no one could have imagined them to have been capable of uttering such angry threats, or of trading blows like rough farmhands, with their coifs in disarray and their honor lying on the floor. Seeing them so submissive and well-behaved, one might have hoped for an election as quiet as many another before it, with the result of the secret vote well known beforehand, a peaceful handing over of the office from one sister to another, more for reasons of health and age than for some other motive born of fierce passions.

The principal cause of the violent contention capable of destroying the harmony of the house now appeared however, arriving amid the others, with her hands bandaged and her veil thrown back over her shoulder, thus baring her true face to us. It was that face that I had seen before, that I had so often held between my hands, paler now and more delicate, with a bold, intense look of hauteur, taking her place in her stall like a queen accompanied by her ladies-in-waiting, amid the commotion caused by her companions' entrance.

They too prayed, though only for a brief moment. Then,

III

barely giving them time to seat themselves, the prioress murmured:

"Very well; let us begin."

She looked round about her like a shepherd keeping careful watch over his flock, and folding her fingers together so
that her two hands looked like a tightly closed pine cone, she
began:

"Ladies, mothers and sisters: I am of the opinion that we
have had more than enough speeches. All of you are aware
of the reason why we are gathered here together. Three years
ago you elected me prioress of this house for the fourth time,
and in those three years I have done my best to serve it and
you as faithfully as my strength has permitted. . . ."

She broke off for a moment, pondering the words that
would follow. No one raised any objection; no one brought
up any of the accusations against her so endlessly discussed
in those nocturnal meetings. No one paid much attention to
this speech that all of us knew almost by heart, a mere orna-
ment and formality, a prelude of the voting that would be a
real measure of the forces for and against the Mother Superior.

"But the years go by more quickly than we anticipate. There
is no term of office that does not come to an end; the march
of time is relentless. In like manner, there is no such thing as
certain happiness, nor any unchanging order of things. Three
years are as nothing, although in recent days unusual happen-
ings, and to a certain extent extraordinary ones, have taken
place in this house. But neither such occurrences, nor any
other reason save the good of the community should guide
the decision that we are about to make today. We are gathered together here to elect a new prioress; a worthy, capable,

pious prioress able to rule over this flock for the glory of God and the greater honor of one and all."

She advanced several paces to the center of the room where the wooden ballot-box had been placed, and after the traditional prayer on such occasions, the sisters were requested to cast their votes. They were handed to her one by one, and with each name that she read, her face paled and her fingers grew less dextrous. A voice requested that the votes cast be read aloud, but there was no need to do so; the balloting was barely half over and already the saint was the new prioress, amid the rejoicing and clapping of hands of her followers. The others, as though beleaguered and certain now of their defeat, had formed a circle about the former prioress, and at that moment were as irate as she was. For a moment we feared another confrontation, the prelude to open battle, as in the days just past, but in the end only insults were traded, although they were grave ones, more befitting ruffians in the street, whereby my sister was called a liar, and crude threats were made to denounce her to the bishop if she did not refuse the office. But she was not cowed by them, nor did she even appear to hear them. On the contrary, serene and secure amid her supporters, haughtily aloof and above all of us, far from me since I did not dare to approach her, she offered thanks to God for such an unexpected honor, so long yearned for.

After that, many days went by in which my soul was weak and wan. My sister's new absence rent my heart, leaving me so distressed and lonely that neither prayer, nor choir, nor labors about the house were able to make me forget that new and grievous purgatory. Love, like fire, is not easily extinguished when it is a great one. Rather, trials and adversities fan it, whereupon the harder one tries to put it out, the more furiously it burns, and laments and prayers are of no avail. It is not an empty word; it is pain, cruel torment, helplessness.

Thus my efforts and passion profited me nothing, and it was of no use to mistreat my body when my soul was already mortified. I needed only to close my eyes and she immediately appeared before me, clothed in the attributes of her new rank, glorying in her recent ascension in the hierarchy. Her new dignity caused me, at one and the same time, to take pleasure in it and to suffer from it, as had her beauty in bygone days, when I had begun to regard her as a real saint, capable even of working all those miracles that people outside the walls kept clamoring for more and more insistently.

Seeing her as distant from me as the Lord's elect must be from other mortals, I began to think that it would better if I were to disregard my faintness of heart and confront her face to face as in the past.

This time I hastened to her cell in full daylight, at the hour when the other sisters had gone out to work in the garden. I went and knocked at her door as I always had, but the sound of violent words being exchanged left me standing there outside, silent and rooted to the spot. I recognized the voice of the former prioress, locking horns with my sister, both of them furious, as though some long-rankling secret animosity between them had finally burst out into the open. As far as I could make out the saint had surprised the prioress searching for something among her garments and had ordered her out of her cell, but the old nun was refusing to leave. As their voices rose, with my sister threatening and cursing her, the prioress's words came out more slowly, ugly and impassioned, intended to wound rather than to persuade by proofs and reasoned arguments. I soon heard what it was that she had been searching for: that little knife with which I myself had begun the deception, and perhaps the means whereby the saint's wounds had later been deliberately kept from healing. And not only was our former prioress furious at not having found anything to confirm her suspicions; she was covered with shame as well at having been caught in the act.

"I'll have Your Charity know," she exclaimed, "that this election will not be confirmed. I shall write to the provincial myself. Either my word counts for nothing or I shall see you excommunicated for having lied before God and the sisters."

"As far as I am concerned, you may take up your pen this minute it it so pleases you. The election has been confirmed and neither the provincial nor a multitude of prelates will be able to quash something that has been decided upon by vote."

"I'll have you banished to another house."

"Does it cause you such pain to see me in this one?"

"It pains me to see you deceive the community in this manner."

"Such words neither offend me nor do me harm. What is more, I willingly forgive you for them. I have no time to waste now listening to threats. Go therefore and join the other sisters."

Everything was silent for a moment on the other side of the door. Then there came to my ears the sound of stifled sobs. In fear and trembling, I impatiently pushed the door open. There at my feet was the old prioress, as painters depict the Devil at the feet of Our Lady—her spirit broken, weeping, covered with dust, and her face bathed in tears. Seeing me in turn, she managed to struggle to her feet, but only with the greatest of difficulty, refusing the helping hand I offered her. She shook the dust from her habit and straightened her coif and veil, casting one last threatening glance at my sister, who appeared to have already forgotten that confrontation and all the words that had gone before.

"This whole farce of your wounds will soon come to an end," the former prioress muttered as she left. "Even if I am obliged to appeal to Rome."

Then all we heard was the echo of her footsteps dying away, and later on, as always, the murmur of the water flowing into the irrigation ditch and the distant sounds of the city borne on the wind. Finding myself face to face once again with my sister, I didn't know whether to embrace her as in the past or whether her new office separated us even more than the many long days that had gone by. But seeing me hesitate, she broke through the mute sense of protocol that held me back, and coming over to me, flung her arms around me, first taking care to shut the door. Pleased and happy, she told me how proud and gratified she was to see how zealously I had kept our secret, how well things were going with regard to the plan we had worked out together, that held every promise of furthering the fortunes of the community and bringing it untold glory, and of procuring us every manner of favor.

For the first time in many a day, I saw her brimming with happiness and in high spirits and, to my misfortune, ready and willing to go even further now.

She told me that for some time now, ever since the news of her wounds had become common knowledge, her soul had continually fallen into sweet raptures. It was as though it dwelt in another world, so far away from everything that she could scarcely make out the faces of the other sisters round about her, or anything else save her own hands. She remained in this state for days at a time, as though she had lost her powers of reason, amid a vast solitude, her soul no longer her own, seized by ecstasies of joy.

I thought that this might be the work of the Great Deceiver, ever prowling about with hallucinations in his bag of tricks, never giving ground; I thought, moreover, that taking advantage of the difficult days that the convent was going through, he was again trying to separate us. The moment such words were out of my mouth, she came to me again, sobbing now, and once more in that quiet little haven of peace, we found each other again, the two of us became one again, our imperishable passion flowering anew.

The world was blotted out, the cloister vanished, the pulse at my wrists and temples that had lain dormant for so long quickened, and my life's blood seemed to overflow its natural channels at the muffled sound of her breathing, to the rhythm of the soft, delicate brushing of her body against mine. My love-sick soul sought its usual remedy in the warm refuge of her arms, its essential nature that would elevate it above all other earthly loves. Nothing held me back this time, no grille, no door stood in my way. My flesh was no longer a heavy weight, but instead a light winged flight in search of a nesting place in which to deposit caresses and tender affection. Body and soul were conjoined, took their pleasure in a secret game which, like a painful dart, pierced our hearts, uplifted them in exaltation, and united us for life.

The memory of so many days, long gone now, of so many

nights of suffering the torture of waiting, was exalted in its turn, no longer hurtful and violent, but happy and loving, its firm foundation the person of the saint. There at her feet I vowed to serve her, to obey her, night and day, in the time to come.

There then came a calm, serene peace, a repose of our bodies, an awakening of our souls such as those who dwell in heaven must feel. But just as the soul raised by love above abandonments and afflictions soon falls back into this vale of sorrows, so our consciences accused us once again, rebuking us for that joyous love, that happy time. Was it not to offend God to take pleasure without suffering, to be aware only of the enjoyable aspect of our flesh? It seemed like a grave sin to make Him share our love through suffering, our pleasure through the chastisement of the flesh. Yet only in this way would we be able, according to the oft-repeated preachings of the saint, to arrive at that fervently desired union with Him who, as our father and our servant, knew passion and tears alike, at once loving and suffering.

And so, as had happened so many other times, my sister leaned over the bed without a word. Having bared her back from the waist up, where I could see the sharp points of her cilice, she held out her hemp scourge to me, begging me to proceed as usual. And as had happened so many other times, as when the former prioress condemned us to a similar chastisement, that tender flesh of hers and mine, a garden of delights, a *via dolorosa,* gradually turned into a field of blood-red furrows. At each blow, body and bed shuddered; I closed my eyes, feeling in my own body the pain of those fine strands, the black and blue marks they left, that would linger for such a long time on that soft flesh. And yet, little by little, the fury of my arm grew. This was to fight love with love, pain with pain, to mortify, to hate her body so that it might be born again, a strange pleasure, a chastisement with the vain hope of feeling it on my own body, while those hands clutching the wooden frame of the pallet struggled to remain motionless as she bore up under the pain of the scourge descending through the air with a dull whisper.

When the blood-red scourge came down on my back, when my sister's hands became in turn the delight and the tormentor of my flesh, the two of us, more united in our carnal rapture and our souls than ever, became as one in a single sob like a flame of love that had transported us beyond this world of mortals.

Afterwards my sister went over to the embrasure of the window that overlooked the wall and removed a handful of jagged shards of glass from amid the dust. She put them in the palms of her hands and for a few instants pressed them tightly together, as though in prayer, until she nearly fainted. In a moment a dark trickle mixed with the dust ran down from between her fingers, a river of mud or a fountain of blood. Then she put her hidden weapon away once more in the window recess, and again, the bandages back in place and the two of us fully dressed, calm and serene, we walked together in silent complicity down the path that the bell was summoning us to follow.

Chapter Four

I N the days immediately following the election, the life of
the house changed little. My sister's fame, on the other
hand, became greater and greater. There were more and more
visits and gifts, a day never went by without a number of
devout on the other side of the turning-box, and on occasion
dense throngs of people, begging for some keepsake, a talisman, an image of the saint. At times she would favor them
with her presence, at times she conversed with women and
those who were ill, but she still refused to allow people to
touch her with medals and crosses, or to promise cures, for
fear of disillusioning them.

Nonetheless that Christmas season was quite different from
ones that had gone before. We had not yet been able to repair roofs and windows, but what rained down on us was
fruit and meat of all sorts, sweet wine and soft marzipan that
took us back to happier days. Even the church became as
animated as it had once been. Long lines of people, caravans
of the pious arrived from the city, as though on pilgrimage,
in part to make their devotions and at the same time with
the hope of seeing, if only at a distance, the new prioress

whose reputation as one who walked in the path of the Lord and could work miracles was spreading like wildfire. Rich and poor, the sick and the healthy, people on foot, humble laborers came, each of them seeking her grace or a return to health after long months of tertian fevers.

A whole defeated horde arrived like a January wind, both fearful and persistent, patiently enduring the chill breath of the snow, building bonfires at which to dry out their clothes and their bones, and at the same time laying siege to us in the hope of receiving favors. Those with means were usually given a prompt reply, returned to their lodgings at nightfall, and then scattered to the four winds. But the others, far more numerous, remained outside the walls, many of them trembling with fever, huddled up next to each other, shivering from the cold as they waited for my sister to show herself, in order to touch her habit if only for an instant, to hear her voice, to try to grasp the firm edge of her hands which would make the mute speak, the blind see, the crippled walk.

One day very early we received an unexpected visit. The news soon spread through the house, greeted by some of the sisters with tears and by others with laughter: like a prodigal daughter, that lay sister who had been my companion on the journey to my father's house had returned. She arrived greatly changed, the shadow of her former self, as though worn out and thoroughly dispirited after many a stupid adventure, abandoned, as I learned later, by that bold friar who had snatched her away from us. She looked so slovenly and unkempt that the portress barely recognized her; the former prioress, my recently elected sister, and I myself had the same difficulty. We had never seen a more miserable creature, or witnessed a more pitiful scene as she humbled herself, wept, fell face downward at the saint's feet, begged to be taken back into the house. The look of amusement and surprise on the other sisters' faces was a sight to behold, since they had no idea what the great faults were for which she was begging forgiveness, what new absolution she had come to seek from our father confessor.

I had revealed nothing on my return to the house; just a few casual words, as though in passing, to the effect that she had stayed behind at her parents', but for some reason the sisters seemed to have guessed what stupid misadventures had befallen her, and once they came to light, they reveled in them. They called her a latter-day Mary Magdalene who had fled to the desert to wash away her sins, to enjoy in solitary rapture her contemplation of her Beloved. "What sweet moments of pleasure!" they said to her, speaking up from behind her back. "How your heart must have leapt for joy amid the crags and brambles! What ardent, arduous nights, so close to the starry heavens, stripped of mortal flesh, sleeping in the mansions of paradise!"

My friend the lay sister didn't know whether to laugh or cry, so derisive was the tone of voice of the others, so mocking the expressions on their faces, though apparently so full of loving charity. She was taken back into the house and assigned the most demeaning tasks: sweeping what no one else swept, emptying what no one else emptied, dumping out and washing the basins in which those sisters who were sick relieved themselves. She accepted everything without the slightest complaint, the least protest, not even when her companions passing by jostled her unexpectedly so that she spilled her bucket of water or walked on the floors that she had just scrubbed or stealthily kicked dusts and clods of dirt on the clean laundry that she had spread out to dry among the trees in the orchard.

Each one of these trials was a silent battle for her, which she won by humbling herself even more, hunching her head down between her shoulders, scrubbing, polishing flagons and candelabra, saying not a word, as though comforted by such self-abnegation.

Moved to pity one day by such severe and continual penitence, I asked her if she would not have a better life outside the walls, leaving behind her the memory of her past missteps. In any event, not everyone was like her friend the friar; there must still be pious people with whom she could associate and serve the Lord without being obliged to suffer such punishment. After all, she had not yet taken the major vows and hence she was free to leave the convent.

My good lay sister stopped dead in her tracks on her way to the kitchen before answering me. She laid down the bundle of firewood she was carrying and murmured, barely raising her eyes:

"However badly they treat me here, I would not return to the outside world even if I had to gather a hundred loads of wood like this one each and every day. Better a humble occupation than a wicked life. There are base people everywhere, but in all my days I have never met anyone worse than that friar with whom Your Charity is acquainted."

"He didn't seem so at the time however."

"That is so, I grant you, fool that I am, but even fools are punished. What with one misery or another, with age and experience everybody eventually learns where the shoe pinches. As for the friar you mention, I hope that the Lord hasn't forgiven him and that he's rotting in hell this very minute."

"That, sister, is to lack charity."

"Charity, you say?" she retorted, in an angrier tone of voice now. "Is it charity to gather a flock of women about him the way the Turks do? That's the sort of charity he showed me after I left this house to follow him, a place where there's at least a clean bed and warm food and even a hole reserved for me in a corner of the cemetery."

"What? You didn't have all that when you were with him?"

"Shared with a whole flock of other women, as I said. That was the drop that made my cup of bitterness run over. Even though it's a plain and humble one, it can hold only so much. It wasn't his words that did it—I never understood them and they didn't matter—but the fact that he put me together with other women, like a harlot in a harem."

She fell silent, sighing, as though reflecting for a moment, before disappearing from sight once again beneath her big unwieldy bundle of birch faggots and heading into a grove of holm-oak trees that scratched her face and shed its leaves all over her wool habit.

She seemed all of a sudden to forget her labors, the friar, the house, and her cruel companions, and in a quiet tone of voice born of so many lost days, so much ill-treatment and wretchedness, went on to tell me how her life with the friar had little by little turned into a purgatory, how he had eventually abandoned her, taking up with other, younger women in her place. In a calm voice, without anger or passion, with no hint of rancor and no trace of sadness, she told me that day, and at other times later on, how after much wandering about by day and taking pleasure by night, begging for food and lodging in convents and the homes of laymen, they had eventually ended up in a city where her companion had a goodly number of old friends, all of them more or less secularized, renegade friars who had fled from their communities and were now wandering about, wild and carefree.

All of them lived an apparently austere life in the secular world, subjecting their bodies to harsh discipline, to every sort of mortification, preaching the virtues of fasts and prayers, but when once they went off together by themselves, like a flock of lustful crows, they revealed themselves in their true colors to the disciples who joined them, in greater numbers with each passing day.

All of them, clerics and lay people alike, would gather, usually in a sacred place, and couple indiscriminately, without distinction of age, sex, or social condition, abusing each other's bodies until amid fainting fits and mad flights of the imagination they were overcome by intense pain, consumed by all sorts of loves and passions that reduced them to insensibility, bathed in sweat, brutalized by pleasure like satisfied demons, like lascivious animals.

Night after night, amid the homage of women who joined them and sermons that she barely understood, amid games and secret ceremonies, her friend's vanity grew, becoming so contagious that there was talk of sending the pope a report requesting that His Holiness officially authorize such ceremonies. His self-confidence, his pride were such that he compared himself to the greatest saints. But before they could send such a petition to Rome, the Holy Tribunal caught up with them, opening an inquiry, taking the clerics in particular into custody, whereupon the latter soon informed against their best pupils.

And it was no doubt the Lord, He who watches over those whom He does not wish to see doomed to eternal perdition, who separated my friend from the friar, and who allowed the latter to be trapped by his own subtle maneuvers on seducing one of the many women who had hastened to listen to the nonsense that poured forth from his lips.

This woman and the friar soon began living in sin together, abandoning the others, who thereafter were more like servants than companions. And so it was that when the imprisonments and trials began, the lay sister, who had parted company with the sect, was let off free, whereas our friar, along with the other clerics forsaken by the Lord, received the first whiplashes of their torture; a clear sign of divine providence, and at the same time a grave risk confronting any woman who trusts men's words.

But there was another reason, as compelling as all the foregoing, responsible for the lay sister's return to this house of hers that she had never completely forsaken or forgotten. And that reason was a new disaster that threatened after the joyous days that followed the end of the drought. Seeing the sickness go away and the long hoped-for rains arrive, people everywhere raised their voices in hymns and prayer, the statues of the saints began to watch over the faithful once again, and the earth seemed to come to life once more in a single, ardent act of thanksgiving.

But when spring came round, the same thing happened as on previous occasions. It soon became evident that no one had bothered to sow the fields, that out of a combination of listlessness and disillusionment, seeing how little care heaven took of them, people preferred to ask for charity rather than sowing grain, to beg for the bread that they took no trouble to grow the wheat for, remembering other years when they had harvested nothing. And since there were very few who

127

possessed seed gain, they would sell it only at exorbitant prices, precisely because they were not receiving their tenth share of the harvest on lands they owned. Hence the roads and the cities were full of idlers, some for lack of ambition and others for lack of resources.

That new universal misery—rich men with seed and barren uncultivated land, and poor men without grain—was becoming even more evident now that the springs were overflowing, washing over fallow fields covered with weeds rather than with ears of grain and grazing cattle. That was a time of hordes of alms-seekers, who almost before day dawned, came each morning to voice their pleas at our gate, and once their needs were satisfied, hobbled on toward other charitable houses. Sometimes, early in the morning, the portress found a nameless infant abandoned there by its brothers and sisters or its parents, or an old man on the point of delivering his soul to God, or invalids of every age and station, whose one request was to be given a corner in which to await his or her end.

In a very short time, and as though the afflictions that had gone before had unexpectedly turned out to be merely a prelude and a foreshadowing of the ones people were suffering now, the world round about us became a dark and somber one once again. Just as we were expecting a much-deserved respite, that world turned hostile and even cruel once more, for as some of the older sisters said, the calamities visited upon us by the Lord are always repeated before they cease to plague us once and for all.

Nonetheless, not everything was the same as before. The roads did not look deserted now; instead, they teemed with beggars, prostitutes, and even false prophets who swept the weakest off their feet and dragged them along after them.

We could hear them from behind our latticed windows, haranguing their pitiful flocks at the tops of their lungs. They inevitably promised them a happy life after death provided they had made a common and public act of confession. And I asked myself how those miserable bands of the blind, the lame, the halt, and the mad could have offended God, what sin, however venial it might be, was within their powers, what they owed to anyone save life itself, that cruel succession of days without a trace of charity round about them, placing their every hope in their faith alone, if not in their wrath. For there were other prophets whose eyes were fixed not on heaven, but on the wealth of the rich, on their prodigality, on their fine garments that they still decked themselves out in for gala occasions. There was one of them who goaded his faithful on to follow him to the very walls of the city, burning houses, destroying everything of value they chanced upon, attacking granaries and storehouses, until men-at-arms come from the court managed to drive them off, having first hanged the ringleaders.

The king's highway was still there as well. Along it, leaving clouds of dust behind them, came those traveling alone, and corteges that cast enormous moving shadows, like huge birds, over the fields as dusk fell.

Royal couriers heading for the court also passed by, barely halting in the city to rendezvous with the horse and rider ready and waiting to take over from them. Almost the moment they disappeared beneath the great arch at the gateway to the city, covered with mud and bone-weary, their comrade

129

would suddenly appear, sitting tall in the saddle and his feet in the stirrups, having just risen from the table or roused himself from sleep, cleaving the afternoon air with his hurried gallop, holding down his hat with his right hand. What news could they be bringing the king? What could they be telling him about these dead lands?

And then they would gallop off, propelled by the night breeze that was rising, by the rays of a sun about to disappear beneath the horizon, headed for other highroads and other walls, ones not made of adobe brick or stone but of silver and gold, those of many a noble house.

But those couriers who were bringing our king news of his towns and villages in the sealed papers in their saddlebags also had ears to hear, eyes to witness, a tongue with which to communicate to friends what was happening, both close to court and far away. Thus it was that we learned that incidents involving the false prophets were not proving easy to end by means of the rope and the stake, that even those of modest means were refusing to pay tribute, fleeing in armed bands to the mountain fastnesses.

Each one according to his need, according to how relentlessly he was pursued by hunger or the tax collectors, chose to the best of his understanding one of these only two possible paths. And rumor even had it that some preferred to die at the hands of the king's troops rather than see death slowly approaching, week after week, without anyone being able to help them, surrounded as they were by friends and relatives living on whatever alms that convents such as ours could give them.

Such was the state of affairs when my sister received a letter from the duke who was our benefactor. In the beginning, the community feared that the letter was bringing us the news that his favors were at an end, but very shortly, summoned to the chapter room, we learned that he intended not only to continue to bestow his favors upon us but to enhance them with that of his presence, promising to visit us in the near future. After having been abandoned for so long, after being merely one more bead in the rosary of his devotions, his reason for remembering us was surely none other than the saint, whose name must have already reached the court, having perhaps been mentioned by some illustrious townsman of the nearby city. He himself acknowledged that this was the reason for his visit in a few scrawled words added below his signature, informing us that he would be pleased to kiss her hands.

Like the Glad Tidings of the Holy Book, the exciting news immediately spread like wildfire, both outside our walls and in the gloomy streets of the city. For an entire week the living forgot the dead, the destitute their wretched existences, and one and all their past disputes. The days of wrath or prayer turned into hectic ones of sweeping, whitewashing, mending, airing tapestries and hangings bearing coats of arms in the sun, while beyond the river, on the battlements of the city walls and along the riverbanks, as on previous great occasions, artificers come from other towns set up their fireworks castles, their small mortars, their skyrockets.

As the appointed day drew near, the hustle and bustle, the new prioress's orders, the enthusiasm of the most devoted of her followers among the sisters and the spitefulness of the others, the veiled insults of the former prioress increased the tension in the air. Some of the sisters even went so far as to accuse my sister of wanting to win the good will of our benefactor at the price of sacrificing the house, of forgetting the hunger of so many poor placed by Our Lord God beneath our protection, of seeking glory and fame by way of her wounds.

In a few days' time, the convent was spotlessly clean, the chapel decorated and ready, the chapter room in perfect order. From the city there arrived daily evidences of the thoughtfulness of the townspeople: lambs, hens, bacon, milk-fed capons, rabbits to offer our patron—and a fair number of doubloons. All of these contributions at a time of such desperate hardship offended some of us, but no one, even outside the house, muttered a single word of reproach, so eagerly were all of us awaiting this unexpected visit, from the lay sister to the saint, whom I had never seen so certain of her authority, so energetic, and so hardworking.

When everything on both sides of the river was all ready—arches, rockets, garlands, viands—the king's highway was clear of traffic, with not a single horseman or cart in sight. The flocks remained on the hillsides, closely watched by the shepherds, and in like manner the clerics kept watch from their towers and the townsmen from the rooftop terraces of their houses. One and all, each according to his self-interest or his needs, awaited the great cloud of dust, or if the journey turned out to be a nighttime one, the moving torches signaling that the great cortege was approaching.

For an entire week everyone waited in vain. Our benefactor's arrival was delayed, and those whose existence depended on our charity but who in the hope of more lavish favors had moved from our walls to the edges of the highway, returned to our house to importune us with their plaintive cries.

But on the eighth day, the churchbells of the city began

pealing at the break of day, obliging us to hurry reluctantly through matins and go post ourselves at the windows.

A cortege was slowly approaching along the main highway. The journey must have been long and exhausting, for it was only as dusk was falling and the day ending that another pealing of the churchbells and the sound of horses' hoofs announced that the long-awaited visit was at hand. As it gradually appeared, the party was seen to stretch farther and farther into the distance, a brilliant procession of horsemen all clad in bright-colored uniforms covered with dust.

That gorgeous caravan was creeping along as slowly as worms in the garden, filling the road with shining arms, bringing more people out onto the nearby hilltops and the walls than we had ever seen before. It was as though the king, our sovereign, himself were arriving in all his majesty, as though the entire court with its ministers and counselors were accompanying him on his journey; and it was as though the countryside, the city, the convent were also about to be transfixed by the passage of that cortege, so great was its pomp and ceremony.

The bells rang out as they must in heaven, the warm wind blew gently, the sound of cheers and rumbling carts rose above the solemn chanting of hymns. When the cortege disappeared behind the walls of the city, the nearby hills suddenly became deserted, the river crept up higher along its banks as hordes of people forded it, and the king's highway suddenly was too narrow to accommodate the great human avalanche struggling to get closer to the walls.

That same night the entire city was set aglow by the great display of rockets set off in the main square. Then many other set-pieces were lighted down by the riverside, leaving in the breeze a smell of burnt cane frames and gunpowder that kept many of the sisters not accustomed to such spectacles wide awake with excitement.

After each burst of fireworks they asked:

"And when will he be coming *here?*"

"Why is His Excellency stopping in the city? It's this house that he's come to visit, this house that brought him here. Don't we count for more than the city?"

"Who knows? It's more than likely that he has other business to attend to there. They say that people are refusing to pay taxes."

"And why is he accompanied by an armed escort?"

"It's the same one he always has with him."

"The one befitting his station?"

"No, sisters, I've never before seen him with such a large pack of men-at-arms."

"Nor has Your Charity ever seen him without them."

"That's true. This is the first time he's come here since we've been in the house. In any event he errs by favoring the city rather than us with his presence. The saint is here, however much some people might wish that she weren't, and no matter how many business affairs may tempt him to linger in the city, he'll be obliged to put them aside sooner or later."

Such talk filled the empty hours as the convent waited. We whiled away the time in idle conversation, and my sister's efforts to keep us away from the latticed windows were of no avail. In answer to the questions of the youngest sisters all she could recommend was that they be patient, assuring them that our benefactor would surely be arriving soon—and not exactly with empty hands, but ready to fulfill the generous promises conveyed by his letter.

But he did not appear on the following day either. In vain

we waited all morning long; in vain we kept our eyes peeled all afternoon, working on our embroidery only with the greatest reluctance. Even my sister could not sit still for long without searching for an excuse to get up from her chair and walk over to the window, without asking our lay sister as darkness fell what news might have come from the city, where apparently the visitor was being accorded one honor after another. It was thus we learned of his arrival at the main church, and then at his own palace, where for an entire day he received all those who came to him with their complaints and requests, giving proof of his devotion and charity for other religious establishments in the city which appeared to have precedence over us.

As for our house, there was only one reason impelling him to visit it: to see, to touch, to kiss the saint's hands, to ask her for good fortune and courage in the undertakings of every sort that our Sovereign King entrusted to him, above all the one that beyond the city appeared to be the most important one of all. For rumor had it that a province even more wretched than ours, half-starved and impoverished by the excises on goods, was up in arms and refusing to pay any of the royal levies, with people preferring to lay waste to their own fields rather than sow crops to pay for cavalry and foot soldiers to carry on other wars still more ruthless and still more remote.

Finally, on the third day, our patron fulfilled the promise he had made in his letter. Very early in the morning people in his retinue came to announce that the long-awaited visit was at hand, and once again all was confusion as the new prioress put on her best habit and all the candles were lighted in the decorated church. As we sisters readied it, we prayed that the duke would not go back on his word, and the Lord must have heard us, for at about tierce, the road that led across the river to our house was lined with strangers and neighbors waiting to see the cortege pass by.

Accompanied by all the sisters of the community, some most willingly and others only out of duty, the prioress came out to receive our patron. The saint stepped forward to offer him the keys of the house, as is the custom on such occasions, but the duke refused them with a vague gesture of exaggerated humility. We all then stood inside the wall watching as our benefactor went inside to the chapter room to pray, occupying the prioress's place. From the choir we stole furtive glances at the elegant, dashing officers accompanying him, their happy faces and gala uniforms, the massive silhouette of his excellency the duke, whose splendid lace-trimmed attire did not conceal the fact that he was beginning to run to fat. His velvet doublet with puffed sleeves and slashed sides barely closed over his bulging belly as his moustachios pointed heavenward and his wide-open blue eyes surveyed in surprise the chinks in the roof or the coat of whitewash peeling away from the damp walls. His appearance and his gestures, his way of moving, kneeling, rising to his feet amid those surrounding him were such that he seemed more like a military captain than a noble courtier. He looked more like a leader of battles than a man of peace, paying little heed to the altar and the choir, his mind on campaigns to come. We thus saw him give a happy sigh of relief when, once the act of thanksgiving was over and he had left his retinue and constables behind, we sisters escorted him to our private reception hall where a collation had been prepared. Once arrived there, my sister, in the name of the community, expressed our gratitude at finding ourselves favored by his presence.

The duke's eyes lingered upon her, no doubt endeavoring to catch a glimpse of her hands hidden in the folds of her habit.

"In point of fact, " he murmured, "I too have been eagerly looking forward to this visit for some time now; above all since the reports of the prodigies that have been taking place in this house reached my ears. Do all of you know that there is talk of them even at court?"

"At court?" A murmur of voices arose among the sisters standing at a respectful distance. "We receive little news from outside here."

Our patron smiled for a moment, and draining his glass of malmsey that our lay sister kept filling every so often with a trembling hand, he added:

"Well, what I say is quite true, and I repeat that had it been left entirely to me I would have come long before, but those of us in His Majesty's service are not always free to do as we would like. We must devote our every hour to him, especially in wartime."

This time we looked at each other in fear. In the shadow beyond the peeling walls we seemed already to hear troops on the march, the sound of sacking and plundering from which not even convents were safe—calamities that had befallen many of our houses. It was true that such depredations always occurred during campaigns against Turks or heretics, yet the tribulations of such a state of affairs spread as swiftly

137

as bad news. But our father and patron immediately set such fears to rest. The enemy he was about to face did not disturb his sleep. This time it was merely a question of a handful of wretched peasants who were refusing to pay the taxes levied by the royal treasury.

"These are hard years," my sister muttered.

And I for my part could have added—I remembered them well—the arguments of that gardener who had taken me and the lay sister to my father's village in his cart.

"The man who tills the soil," he had said, "is obliged to support himself, the owner of the land, the tax collector, and the one who comes for the tithes, because prelates, grandees, and landowners, those who gather in the harvest of the grain that the rest of us have sown, don't pay out anything at all; they merely take in what we who labor in the fields have produced. They don't pay excise taxes because they load them off on our shoulders."

Though I was only a woman without schooling, knowing nothing save what life teaches, those words echoed loudly in my mind as I listened in silence to the duke's explanations.

"For the royal treasury, there are neither good years nor bad ones," he was saying to my sister in reply. "There are only vassals ready and willing to pay it what they rightfully owe it, or else to skimp on paying their share of the expenses incurred by the State in funding the wars that His Majesty wages to uphold the faith in every corner of the globe. The safeguarding of Christendom is a cause well worth being supported by the levying of such trivial sums."

"They are not as trivial as all that, Excellency."

"I might better have said small, since they amount to very little by comparison with other capital that comes from more distant places. But small or not, they must be obtained, for it is not right that some villages help and others refuse to, no matter how stubbornly they rebel or how many popular courts they hold."

"But the latter have always paid in good years."

"And I say that this does not excuse them now," our patron retorted, in an impatient tone of voice this time. "I am planning to leave no later than tomorrow to have it out with them."

What thoughts were passing through my sister's mind as she nodded in silence, like all the others? Was she remembering her parents, who had lost everything they had inherited? She merely stood there without a word, listening to the duke as he explained in his monotonous voice how he would have preferred to lay siege to a fortress and force it to surrender or to fight on the high seas rather then serve his lord and master in such undertakings as the one he was embarking upon.

"It does you as much honor to serve him in modest ones as in lofty or exceptional ones. This is your house, Excellency. As always, it and this community are at your entire disposal."

"That is yet another of the reasons that have brought me here," the duke replied in proud self-assurance, turning his gaze away from the saint for a moment to embrace the whole room. "In view of the news that has reached my ears concerning the prodigies that have taken place in this house, it is my intention to bequeath it, along with the properties appertaining to it, to your community, freeing it in perpetuity of any and every sort of taxes or levies."

A surprised murmur spread through the semidarkness once again. Our chaplain, who thus far had said not a single word, flung himself at the duke's feet, but the latter withdrew his hands, thus cutting off with a brusque gesture the chaplain's impulsive act of devotion.

"There is no need to thank me. It is a small matter to make a donation of four walls when within them such amazing events have taken place. I would be a bad Christian were I not to renounce, to the benefit of these holy women, those privileges which, having come from the hand of Our Lord who giveth all, I merely return to Him by way of another path."

We were all amazed by such a declaration. We would never have thought that such a man, such a great lord, practiced in the avaricious ways of the court, could be capable of expressing himself in such generous terms, but his strong, firm voice had even greater surprises in store for us.

"I too had the intention in my youth of abandoning the world, as the holy books say, and devoting my days to solitary prayer."

Under cover of that soft semidarkness, I struggled to imagine him in the coarse woolen habit of the hermit, living on the charity of others, sleeping among the rocks, drinking melted snow from the hollow of his chubby hand. His silhouette—too plump, too tall, too imposing there amid our mantles and coifs—was at odds with such intentions, with the glances he must have felt round about him in the silence with which these words were greeted. As though appointing our chaplain as the interpreter of our doubts and surprise, he turned to him and repeated:

"All that is quite true. A strong vocation that my daughter has inherited. It and the fame of this house have led her to decide to join a religious order."

"Is she thinking of taking vows?"

"That is her intention at present."

"And what house is she thinking of entering, Excellency?" the chaplain inquired. "A convent under the patronage of the court?"

"Not at all. It is her desire to be a nun in this house."

"Why in precisely this one?"

"Where is there a better one, if one stops to think about it? For once, her decision strikes me as a most reasonable one."

"I wouldn't be the one to deny it; I was merely expressing my surprise."

"And why should you be surprised?"

The chaplain had fallen silent, totally at a loss for words, unable to answer the duke. It was my sister who, in the name of all of us, spoke for him, saying:

"You both surprise and honor us. You surprise us because we thought this house too poor to receive such a noble guest. You honor us because no one of such distinguished lineage has ever before sought refuge among us."

And as she spoke, the saint began walking about, pointing out to the duke the places in the roof where the worm-eaten laths showed through, the broken plaster, the chinks through which the melted ice dripped down once the first spring thaws began. She laid everything before him the way surgeons expose the various parts of an injured body, a doctor the sores of a sick man, or a butcher the entrails of an animal after it has been slaughtered.

As the light of the candelabrum she held penetrated each and every one of the different parts of that great skeleton mortified by so many years of heat and frosts, our patron

141

made a wry face and his manner grew graver and graver as he walked along stroking his leather sword belt with his right hand, as though confronted by a difficult and serious situation, as though prepared to do battle not with stupid peasants rebelling against the king but with hurricane winds, hail, and storms. He became even more irate when he was told about the provincial's report that had struck such fear in our hearts.

"And who is he to decide whether the convent should be closed or not? I shall take whatever steps are necessary, and if need be I shall write to His Majesty with my own hand. You may rest in peace; this house will not be closed as long as I am alive."

Once again there came a murmur from the sisters present, this time one of mingled benedictions and weeping. They offered their thanks to God as the chaplain and the prioress, at a loss for words, looked at each other in silence, as though their every desire had been fulfilled. Finally the saint made a move to kneel like all the other sisters, but the duke stopped her.

"It is I who should kneel at your feet. Allow me, rather, if you insist on thanking me for such a humble favor, to show my devotion by kissing your hands."

I felt my heart sink deep into my breast, closed my eyes in order not to see my sister's nod in assent, and tried not to hear the rustle of her mantle. Amid a hollow silence broken only by sighs that crackled like thunderclaps following upon the bright flashes of the lamp, I heard those two pharisaic hands return to the light from amid the neat folds of her habit, and the breath of the entire community being held behind the veils covering the sisters' faces.

There came from outside the vague din of words being exchanged and loud cries being uttered, the way in which pilgrims, women, soldiers were passing the time and expressing their feelings. Their voices came from another world altogether, a world full of warmth and life, not one frightened and solemn as ours was. It was then that I heard for the first time a voice singing the ballad of the new saint, recounting the story of the principal events centering upon her, which from then on was to haunt me at night, every word of which I contrived to learn by heart, a ballad full of devotion and of extraordinary details invented out of the whole cloth. It was then, on hearing her name being hailed beyond the vines on the walls, the patios, the gratings, that some inner voice told me that the saint was parting company with me, that the upward flight of her spirit was to be different from mine, lofty, deliberate, wary, less simple than mine.

And thus it was that she showed her hands once again, carefully, deliberately, slowly. Little by little she revealed them, as slender as the wings of a hawk, older and more disciplined now, seemingly transparent and livid in places, criss-crossed by those veins whose faintly warm, ashen-colored meanders my lips had so often kissed. Those sweet hands whose love-gestures were so gentle, so burning-hot and fierce when that love came in the dark hours of the night, those hands so docile when they lay unfolded, dead, proud, recognized at their very first touch, ever cold, solemn, painful. They were now seeing the light of day again beneath the circle of agitated veils that barely hid the sisters' anxiety, a certain curious, hesitant, profound uneasiness.

There they were, in the light once more, as they had been the last time, before the eyes of the former prioress. There they were, clean, smooth, neatly groomed, gleaming, with their twin imprints, worked over with the dust and the shards of glass. There they were, ready to bleed once more if necessary, to impart blessings, to divide the community in two, some of the sisters indignant and others humbly acquiescent, but all of them, when all was said and done, happy at the prospect of the good times to come that that ceremony portended.

The duke, for his part, with one knee touching the floor, holding his hat in his right hand, was raising that dead flesh to his lips with his left hand, perhaps believing that he was partaking of the essence of an extraordinary sign, kissing the very wounds of Our Lord, touching his lips to His miraculous blood. His devotion, his faith, his profound rapture was that of a child who kisses his mother's fingertips, his ecstasy, his pleasure, his pride such that upon rising to his feet, he seemed to have made those wounds his own, to have taken to his heart the entire house to which he was about to give over forever that daughter of his in the flower of her young years, our future sister.

When he had rejoined his escort awaiting him at the gate, the ceremonies attendant upon his arrival were repeated once more, this time to thank him for his visit. The promises he had already made were again reiterated, and soon his cortege disappeared from sight amid a cloud of dust, leaving behind it a convent moved to tears. When he entered his coach he appeared to have become his usual self once more, his manner once again grim and severe, his forehead furrowed in a solemn frown, a man accustomed to more lofty undertakings, more momentous concerns.

We sisters remained behind, peeking out from behind the

144

tapestries and latticed windows, awaiting our modest glory, a time certain to come, one of faith and blessings that we divined in the look in the eyes of the former prioress, in the expression on my sister's countenance, in her new demeanor as she left the room, her cup of good fortune running over, and showered with felicitations.

What place was left then for her love for me? For those silences that are the solace of the senses, for that loneliness wherein our melancholy called us to each other and guided our footsteps through cloisters and passageways until we became as one in the innermost depths of our bodies and our souls, like brother and sister, in that passion shared in our wary hours? That great flame that seems to consume and destroy would never again be ours; it was plain to see that our shared wealth of feeling that had given us warmth and life was about to die, so smothered did it appear to be, dimmed by her glory, gravely threatened by her new prominence. Who would be able to approach her now, to follow her every footstep, to die with her each night, lulled to sleep by her dark voice, watched over by her dreams? I was but a poor wretched creature now, mere dust, the most unhappy of all the sisters, abandoned, alone, with nothing to comfort me save her memory and my misery, stored away in my heart now, in the musty attic of my remembrance.

It was that same night, or very shortly thereafter, that our enemy came to visit me. He did not appear in his abominable guise such as it had been described to me since my earliest childhood: I did not see flames all about him, emanating from his very body, nor did I smell brimstone, nor any other sign betraying his identity, save for his eyes that for some reason reminded me of my sister and his mouth as thin as though carved upon his face with a single slash. There was nothing fierce or frightening about him, yet my trembling hand sought the cross about my neck. He told me not to trouble myself, that I was in no danger, and his voice was as loving and vibrant as that of a father speaking to a rebellious child to offer counsel. He told me there was no reason to resist him, and with the tone of voice and the demeanor of a gentleman he expressed great interest in the health and welfare of the convent and my own in particular, as though he did not wish to enter into the heart of such matters without my leave.

I barely answered. When I moved my lips, the words came tumbling out and were immediately swallowed up in the dark; I was thinking only of the moment when those two eyes above the cruel mouth that had now fallen silent would emerge from the dark and his face take on definite form as he brought it closer to mine.

And as I feared, that was precisely what happened, for in a moment or so, divining that my strength was failing me, he made his way toward me very slowly, causing the wooden planks to tremble as he did so. A great gust of mingled terror and passion was suddenly unleashed inside my head, as when in times past I headed for my sister's cell. I thought I was about to suffocate; I tried to scream but his icy hand sealed my lips so tightly that I was left insensible, overcome with an acute stabbing pain that as it pierced my body was at once unbearable and most pleasurable. That sweet dagger buried in my side deprived me of my last remaining powers of reason. That new pain, a commingling of love and the rapture of the senses, was such that finally my anguish exploded within my breast, causing my vocal chords to burst into a moan that echoed far beyond the silence of the cloister.

When I opened my eyes once more, the darkness seemed pitch-black and empty as before, but at the same time alive with echoes and the sound of voices approaching from outside. Some of the sisters were asking if the moaning had come from one or another of the cells; others were calling for lights; and most of them were attributing the groan to a sister's bad dream, as though they were eager to return to whatever activities my cry had interrupted, as though they were frightened by their own fear.

The door finally opened part way. In the gleam of light that a hand extended, the doorway was filled with whispers and discreet questions. And among the throng of sisters, I thought I discerned my enemy once again, still lurking about. I did my best to warn my sisters but they paid no heed to me. I tried to rise to my feet but as I leaned on the straw pallet for support, my legs, weak and drenched with sweat, gave way beneath me.

I began to scream. It seemed to me that I was surrounded by a great, burning brightness, a profound desire to go to meet that friendly shadow. That flame, that fire, at once the object of my ardent desire and my enemy, erased from my mind all memory of my words, my complaints, my pains, that anguished fear of dying, that self-torment. I felt him so close to me that I could make out his eyes. There were not surly, morbid, or cruel, but quite the contrary: wet with tears, serious, sad, as though gazing beyond death, mayhap at his own inferno or the eternal glory he had lost at the very beginning of time.

And then suddenly the pains, the fear of dying, the anguish of my soul, the nausea of my flesh abated. A peace now where nothing existed, where nothing reached me save clear bright

147

light and that sweet, soft sadness surrounded me, penetrated me, wiped away my sweat, seemed to restore life to my battered body.

Never did I regret so much as on that occasion having to return again to the sad solitude of the cell, never did I fear it so much despite the affection of my other sisters who sprinkled me, like well-fertilized earth, with holy water brought from the church.

And now the remedy mingled with the sweat on my body, with the foam that little by little, I learned, my enemy had caused to come bubbling out at the corners of my mouth.

"She's coming back to her senses," my sisters cried. "The Tempter is gone now," and as they washed me and attended to my needs, I was able to make out the former prioress, who was doing her best to hurry them up and get them out of the cell as quickly as possible.

Once they had cleaned me up and put my garments in order, the two of us were left alone in the cell. She then proceeded to close the door and began to console me, reproaching me for my tears and outcries, wanting to know the reason behind such a grave turn of events. And as I looked into her eyes, I suddenly discovered that they were the same ones that I thought had been driven away. There they were once more, worn, out, empty, not keen and sharp as before, but dulled, though not with anguish but with great dejection. Their gaze fixed beyond my shoulders, they contemplated the wall, the crucifix, the secret corners of the cell.

"May Jesus be with Your Charity," she said at last. "What was it that you were bewailing a while ago?"

In the face of such cold and formal address, I was at a loss to reply.

"There is no one here," she insisted. "No one can cause

you any harm. Come, come, set your mind at rest and answer me."

But my soul, though mute, was on guard, especially with her there before me, as haughty and distant as though nothing had happened, as though that secret between my sister and me were a matter of little moment, an irrelevant subject brought up now merely to fill my silence until I fell asleep at last.

"What was it that Your Mercy saw?" she asked again. "What is it that has so upset you tonight?"

I could only shake my head, feigning a drowsiness that I did not really feel, touching my forehead, my side, my temples, all those parts of my body that still ached.

"So then, nobody came to you? You had no dreams? No apparitions? What was it then? What happened?"

"Nothing that I can remember now."

She looked at me, still distrustful, muttering to herself for some reason:

"It must have been the spirit of God withdrawing, leaving no sign of his passage." Standing at the door now, she added: "Come, come, take heart. Remember that the Lord inflicts only as much pain upon his creatures as they can bear. Not for nothing is it said that his cause is the cause of the weak. It is my hope that the truth will eventually be revealed, and either I am very much mistaken or else the tangled web of lies that the Devil has woven in this house will be swept away, clearing the path for light and obedience."

"That is how it will be," I replied.

"That is my belief too. There will come a time when the just will gather the fruit of their humiliations. Meanwhile, try to sleep. The prioress will excuse you from matins."

But sleep was not to come to me that night; it would not

return so long as I closed my heart to reason, my mouth to the truth, to the path to my salvation by way of the good name and the best interests of the saint. Mayhap the former prioress was not my enemy as I thought; it may well have been that when all was said and done she wanted only the best for me, in exchange for my confession, for just a few words. Mayhap she had come to be my new protectress, my companion in that new loneliness that I was experiencing, in that time of bitter anxiety that I was undergoing.

Her voice now was the voice of my father who had passed on to God's glory, of my mother who was enduring such suffering here below, the voice of my conscience that at once called unto me and reproached me. Seeing her thus disposed, I was suddenly overwhelmed by the thought that I could no longer bear this latest turn of events.

"Sister," I called to her, "I pray you to come here."

"What is it that's come over you now?"

Standing next to my cot once again, she grasped my hands above the fold in the blanket as the saint had done in bygone days.

"I beg you not to leave me alone till dawn breaks."

"Do you want me to summon the prioress?"

"I'd rather you summoned our confessor."

"At this hour?"

"I don't want to die during the night."

"What's this talk of dying when better times are coming for this house? Rest, close your eyes and try to sleep. They say that sleep drives away burdensome memories."

But I did not give in. I seized her by the cloak and like someone seeking not to lose salvation I again begged her not to leave me by myself. Seeing my tears, she must have realized for the first time what a grave crisis I was undergoing, since I was ready and willing to make the confession she so ardently desired. With her good judgment, that had not failed her despite her years, she must have known the direction in which my soul was tugging me, the person who would be implicated by my urge to confess, by my desire to unburden my conscience, thereby somehow redeeming and saving myself.

I was just about to explain to her that I wished to speak of the new prioress when my sister suddenly appeared on the threshold as though summoned there by the thought in my mind, as though drawn there by my weeping. Hastily dressed, her shoes half on and half off, she seemed to be instantly aware of my doubts, of the self-interest of her enemy, of my moment of weakness in her presence. The mere look in her eyes sealed my lips, a mere gesture sufficed to cause her predecessor to withdraw, meekly and obediently, though not willingly.

When the two of us were alone once more, my sister endeavored yet again to woo me with honeyed words, in a voice that recalled old love-bouts, nights of sincerity, shared mortification of the flesh, cruel and painful ties. She must have thought that time was entirely on her side, but her wounds had changed not only those soft hands but her entire body from her feet to her countenance; her gaze was no longer the sister of mine, and even her voice was much harder now, not broken by the ecstasy of pain in those hours when love used to leave us exhausted.

She must have thought that the time that had gone by since was as nothing to me, that I would be quite willing to obey, to respond, body and soul, in that imprisoning embrace of her loving arms, as I always had in the past.

"In the holy name of God! Leave me alone!" I said to her,

and seeing her surprise at such words, I added, in tears: "What more do you want of me? What can I give you that I have not already given you in abundance in days gone by? Please know that I want to leave here forever."

She freed me from her embrace and stared at me in astonishment.

"Where do you want to go?"

"To another house," I answered immediately. "Into the world. Somewhere that I may forget my sins."

Once again she fell into a thoughtful silence, staring at the floor in front of my feet, as though passing judgment on me. Then she said, more to herself than me, in a slow monotone:

"Sometimes sins are the means that the Lord uses to sanctify the soul. What sin have we committed? Is not our body the mirror, the seat, and the kingdom of God? What harm is there in imitating Him, engraving upon it the marks of the wounds He suffered on the Mount of Calvary? If we wish Him to come and bless this house, it must be kept calm and peaceful, untouched by fear. We can only suffer and hope, go to meet Him with our eyes closed, for only faith saves us, above and beyond all our good or bad deeds."

I did not recognize her in these new words, these startlingly new ideas, this vague philosophizing. I could not fathom why she was speaking to me, a humble sheep in Christ's flock, in those veiled words that seemed to point to further deceptions rather than to honest intentions. As she spoke, as her words fell on my ears, rather than feeling her close to me, it seemed to me that with each of her pronouncements and explanations she drew farther away from me.

"What are sins—as Your Charity calls them—but tests to make us more deeply aware of our baseness? Sin tempers our soul if we place ourselves in the Lord's hands. We are nothing save miserable seeds sown broadcast by Him, some of which fall by chance on barren ground and others on fertile soil, there to enhance His glory."

"But it is a sin to lie as we have done. To deceive the community."

"Deceive?" She looked at me with pity in her eyes. "Who are we to judge ourselves, to declare what is false or true? Only He who holds us in His hands can say if we are lying or not, only He can weigh the import of our footsteps."

As the conversation went on, a great gust of wrath arose within me. She was not only endeavoring to confuse me with her false words, but was insulting me by taking me for a fool.

"Oh, no!" I said to her. "Such arguments might sound convincing to others, but I am not taken in by them—I who rent the skin of those two hands of yours, who was your friend and companion for so many nights. Do you no longer remember me? Has so much rapture and delight, such swooning in ecstasy, such delicious pleasure faded so soon from your memory? You have no need of vain words to dismiss me if that be your will. Tell me so straight out, in plain and simple words, and I shall never again importune you. I shall not speak to you or ever look at you again, but let me go somewhere that I do not have to close my eyes in the choir in order to veil my fear and my shame. You will hear no more of me, and rest assured that no one will ever learn anything from my lips, for I will never be capable of denouncing you."

And now her tears flowed freely, now they mingled with mine as we embraced there alone together. Once more, and to my sorrow, our love was reborn amid its barely warm dying embers.

Chapter Five

Y ET another autumn came round with its cortege of winds and its skies filled with slender clouds. Once again everyone hastened to take shelter, with wine and firewood close at hand, awaiting the last season of the year, the one that sweeps away lives and marks the end of the harvests. The couriers traveled up and down the king's highway with their faces shielded from the assault of the sun's last rays and the first crystals of winter frost. Their passage from time to time marked that of the hours more precisely than our belfry; the sound of blind flocks reached us in the moonlight, causing us to seek out our cilices in the semidarkness, if not our mantles and sandals.

Nothing changed for a time, since our protector, surrounded by his cavalry company and his retinue, had journeyed forth to that war of rebellion that his arms and horsemen portended.

As the nights grew longer, the days turned gray and leaden, and the sun set like a broken yellow crystal ball that was reborn each dawn, casting its gaze over the dead fields. It was reborn to the rhythm of the passing hours, more a witness than a judge, watching, like the indifferent stars, to see what the ultimate fate of the house would be, reading our destiny here below, mayhap asking itself what misfortunes we would suffer. Seeing it rise, announcing itself first in the tattered remains of the clouds, in the tops of the elms, in the tense shadows of the hills, it seemed to us to be the gaze of all of Creation, the eyes of the Lord watching over our destiny. Its rays did not bring warm days as in other seasons, but instead long, melancholy afternoons when our hours dragged, dull and empty.

And just as we were again beginning to be dispirited, there finally arrived the long-awaited letters, already forgotten by some of the sisters and feared by others. The news announced in them, so soon to divide us, was that of the imminent arrival of our protector's daughter, that unusual sister whose stay among us had been proclaimed and promised by the father.

It was necessary to ready one of the largest cells, decorating it with tapestries and hangings bearing coats of arms, replacing the humble esparto with wool and velvet, arranging for a solid oak bed, which had fortunately been given us for her, to be brought from the city. Little by little there arrived after it chairs upholstered in satin, soft cushions, a brazier on a gilded stand for the freezing weather already in the offing, and lamps so as to be able to see into cupboards and light up dark corners.

Day after day we kept a close watch on the road via which the father had come, for the new novice would be coming that way as well. Hour after hour we gazed into the distance beyond the cultivated fields, but apart from lumbering farm carts and drowsy flocks, nothing appeared on the horizon, nor did we hear the pounding of horses' hoofs or piercing whistles clearing the way for the approaching company. There followed more days of waiting, of growing impatient, all the more so now that the cell was ready and the community prepared to receive her. And since nothing in this world is immutable, the first complaints were voiced to the saint, not overly hostile ones, but nonetheless reproaching her for all these attentions. According to some of the sisters, the lineage of the novice that we were awaiting was of no importance. It was an offense to the rest of the community to prepare such a grand reception even though it was in our interest to so honor our protector. Someone also pointed out that perhaps our benefactor, evidence of whose good offices had yet to be seen, might not ever come back from that war whose outcome he would never live to see. Perhaps too the daughter might never arrive, and everything would turn out to have been a mere summer shower, or like those rivers whose waters sink underground and never surface again, swallowed up, dry, dead.

It was useless, and a sign of disrespect toward the house, to stop our work every time the lay sister spied a modest mule-team or a company of horsemen in the distance.

The one who spent the most time lost in such daydreams and delusions was in fact our sister the portress, mounting patient guard at the entrance, or else in the belfry, where she was inclined to set the bell to pealing the instant her eyes managed to make out something in the distance, even though it eventually proved to be nothing more than a pack of gypsies.

But our impatience was rewarded at last when one day a group of gentlemen on horseback arrived. They must have

157

spent the night in the city, for very early in the morning, even before the lay sister was at her post, they came knocking very politely on the door to summon the portress. They knew neither the region nor the town nor the community but had found their way by asking directions. They had come from the house of our benefactor to find out whether his daughter's cell was ready. The prioress tried to honor them with as long and ceremonious a collation as possible until, noting the impatience of the eldest of them, she invited them to enter the cloister after warning us to veil our faces and asking them to present the letter in which the bishop authorized their visit.

The oldest of their number, followed by two secretaries, went through the formalities of the visit reluctantly, like men not accustomed to such missions, and listened with ill-disguised impatience to the information offered, quickly returned to their mounts and disappeared up the road once more to join our guest, who was arriving.

The community came out to the entrance to wait for her. The bells were about to ring out, but almost the moment she set foot on the ground, she declared she wanted nothing out of the ordinary to be done for her in the house, making such protestations of humility that we were all left open-mouthed with amazement.

For several weeks her life conformed in every respect to the usual rules and habits of the house. Her manner was so unassuming, her behavior so much like that of the others that her presence was scarcely noticed. Her obedience made her seem like one of the older sisters, ever ready to hasten to lend a hand wherever she was needed. Her zeal, her eagerness not to stand out from the rest of us, was such in those days that her new sisters were already beginning to forget her noble rank; the most friendly of them were pleased, and the most hostile disappointed.

In all truth, none of the difficult situations so gravely feared came to pass, for the new arrival seemed in every way to be just another novice, and already there were those who, seeing such virtues in her, proposed that she take the veil before the date agreed upon, after receiving special permission to do so, which surely the Visitor of our order would not deny.

But it is clear in this world there is no joy that is certain, no good that is permanent. This pleasant state of affairs, this unexpected peace lasted for only a brief time, as new consignments of goods and equipment kept arriving. Her cell, in the earliest days as humble as all the others, little by little was transformed into a luxurious chamber, into a storehouse of cosmetics, finery, furniture. A young personal maid also arrived to serve her and attend her, on the pretext that she too was thinking of taking vows later on, and we sisters were secretly astonished on seeing how sweetly and tenderly they comported themselves with each other, not like mistress and servant but like two intimate friends.

Our passionate eagerness to learn about that new life so different from ours reached the point that at times we took turns visiting them, inventing the clumsiest of excuses, so as to find out more about their tastes and predilections.

Our guest seldom rose at an early hour now; she never saw dawn again, she knew no more of the hard crystals of ice or the slightly warm darkness of the choir or the eternal squabbling of the blackbirds. Just as the sun was rising, as numb with cold as its own rays, the maidservant began to ready her mistress's garments, lit the fire, and poked up the embers in the brazier. As the first light of day peeped through the window, she began to lay out her lady's garments. The latter no longer deigned to wear the habit, as though her cell had been turned into her own royal domain where, as she sat before her mirror of old polished silver, her servant very carefully arranged her hair and eyebrows round about the constellation of her beauty marks. After that she fastened the two wings of her parted hair in place with hairpins as long as poniards, and with liquid from a vial that she kept hidden in the writing desk she painted her mistress all white, from her throat and her breast to the hollows of her palms. Then, before our fascinated eyes, watching all aglow, she applied on top of this layer of white touches of pink that brought a soft blush to her mistress's lips and cheeks, until the latter was satisfied with the transformed face that the silver mirror reflected. All of this in silence, her footsteps measured, her gestures slow and deliberate, like a formal rite, with her shadow as acolyte, that lasted far into the morning.

When I saw all these labors, I understood how she was able to keep her face looking so fresh and bright till evening, whereas we sisters by comparison with her resembled filthy devils, tattered and torn and all worn out.

At about this time my sister, having been asked by our novice to pay her a visit, asked me to accompany her; I do not know whether she requested my company because she would feel more sure of herself if there were two of us, or because her health was again failing and she was feeling weak if not downright ill. Hence though only one of us had been invited, I hastened to go with my sister as though I were her maidservant.

My devotion was amply repaid. I had never had a close look at such an elegant, luxurious, and comfortable private chamber, worthy of such a distinguished guest, and no doubt my sister had never seen the likes of it either. When we entered, neither of the two, mistress or servant, deigned to interrupt the work at hand. The maidservant had just sipped a goodly mouthful of rose water, and blowing it out from between her teeth, was bathing her mistress's face with the perfumed water, filling the air with a fragrant scent as on the feast of Corpus Christi. Only when that shower had ended and dried on her skin and the flagon been put back in the cupboard did our guest turn round and ask the prioress:

"So, then, you've finally decided to pay us a visit? It would seem as though this cell attracts you less than the others."

"It has more the appearance of a palace than a cell," my sister said softly, staring intently at the commode of lignum vitae full of pomades.

That childish queen laughed abruptly.

"What an inadequate idea you have of such noble dwellings!"

"I've never visited one of them."

"I am personally acquainted with a number of them. Including that of His Majesty."

"And what about him? Are you personally acquainted with him?"

"The king?" Before my sister could answer, she replied in her gleeful voice: "He's not any different from other men. He has two hands, two feet, two arms, and, I hear tell, so many estates and dominions that when the sun sets in some of them it's already peeking over the horizon in others." And noting that the prioress's eyes were fixed on the garment that her maidservant was holding out for her, she added: "I see that despite the rules of the order, you are not altogether disdainful of such worldly finery either."

"For the very reason that the rules forbid it, you ought to forgo such costumes."

"It's only a matter of days now before I do so, so you may set your mind at rest. I'm merely waiting till the habit that I ordered arrives — and if I'm not mistaken it's already finished and ready to be delivered. And you may be assured that once I take my vows, I shall be as faithful to them as the best of all my sisters and one day I shall even rank first in every way."

The prioress said nothing in reply. Perhaps she chose not to understand, or perhaps I read into those words a meaning beyond what was actually said. She looked at our queen one last time, and before putting an end to that visit that was somewhere in between a hostile confrontation and a brief conversation, she asked in turn, referring to our guest's young attendant:

"And what shall we do with your chambermaid?"

"The day I take my vows she is thinking of doing likewise."

"Does she have that strong a vocation?"

"Why wouldn't she have? Her greatest desire is to serve me in every way possible," she insisted good-humoredly. "Her life will not be greatly changed by taking the veil."

"It would be better to hear what she has to say about the matter."

"There's little point in doing so. We've been together for so long a time that there will be no need whatsoever to force her." She turned to the girl: "Isn't that so?"

"It's as you say, milady. You know that my life depends on

you. My vocation depends on yours. Do as you please with me, for I will obey you in everything."

The saint and I were amazed at such devotion, and our queen, pleased at such words and haughtier than ever, stood looking down upon us from the height of her toplofty pride. My sister seemed to be at a loss for an answer although, knowing her, I suspected that she was saving her arguments for later, for a second inevitable encounter. We left the two of them in the cell, and once in the cloister, the portress came to meet us. The doctor was asking for permission to enter.

"Are there sick people to attend again?" I asked.

"It's a matter of little moment," the saint answered as she authorized the doctor's visit. "I'm the one who needs looking after this time. Come with me. I don't want it said that I fail to observe the rules of the house."

Her footsteps faltered and her eyes looked like glowing coals beneath her veil; she brought to mind a sick, injured bird as she waited for the doctor, hiding her hands in the dark folds of her cloak.

But the moment he touched her forehead, that honest, upright man asked her to show them to him. He had almost immediately guessed the truth that I feared most, the fact that my sister's malady was the consequence of our sin. When the wounds finally appeared in the light of day, we could see that the poison had spread rapidly. The doctor finished undoing the knots of her bandages, and as he proceeded, the color drained from her face, leaving her so pale that it was necessary to lay her down on her bed.

"You had best rest for a bit. There is no need to hurry now."

Struggling to maintain her composure, the prioress muttered a few words:

"I did not send for you before because at other times I have been able to overcome these pains. But it's different now. There are nights when I can neither keep vigil nor sleep; they're like two daggers that pierce my bones and tendons through and through."

"Let us see what they look like."

Our doctor went on with his task, and the remaining bandages finally came undone and fell onto the bedcovers. As the poison and the red traces it had left gradually came to light, the linen bandages bore darker and darker stains, and a foul smell, not particularly noticeable at first, began to rise from the flesh wounds in her hands. The doctor's frown matched the prioress's look of pain that grew more somber, darker, more concerned by the moment, as his fingers came closer and closer to the putrid flesh, to the blood that had turned into trails of hard clots.

When one of those blood stains, at one time a clean wound, emerged in the light with its unmistakable color of putrefaction, none of the three of us present spoke a single word, not even my sister, who was awaiting his verdict in fear and anguish, concealed only with the greatest effort. She merely stared intently at the doctor, trying as I was to read the verdict in the look in his eyes, his motionless lips, his fingers that little by little were lightly exploring the dead edges, the clusters of little broken veins, doing his best not to graze that great dark eye, that black lagoon that was the source of the poison.

"Have they looked like this for some time?"

"I don't remember. A month perhaps, a few weeks."

164

"Only a few weeks?"

"I don't remember very well. Let us say two weeks, a month. When I don't have a fever, I forget about them."

The doctor was lost in thought again, as silent as before.

"You had best summon the chaplain."

"The chaplain would be of no help. He has no knowledge of such things, not being a doctor," my sister answered.

"And I for my part have no knowledge of supernatural causes. What knowledge I have, as you well know, I acquired in this world here below, above all on the battlefield. I have no desire to find fault with those who have already determined the cause of these wounds."

"The cause matters little now," my sister replied. "The one thing I seek now is an end to this pain."

"I shall try to relieve it insofar as I am able, though I warn you that the remedy is a drastic one. Pain is alleviated only by pain, and in the case of these miraculous hands I can think of no more effective treatment than cautery."

The doctor's words made the prioress tremble. As she allowed him to probe the wounds to determine how far the poison had spread, she appeared to be placing her trust in Our Lord God and praying that the verdict would be favorable. The doctor for his part had taken out of the satchel that he had brought with him a silver needle, as long as a sigh and as sharp as the fear that little by little was penetrating our flesh. With it he pricked the palms of her hands, the balls of her thumbs, her fingers, her arms up to the elbows, looking intently the while into my sister's eyes, seeking in them a more certain and more honest answer than the one forthcoming from her lips.

"Does Your Mercy feel anything?"

165

"Nothing. . . ."

"And now?"

"Even less. Nothing whatsoever."

He withdrew the needle and put it back in its lined wooden case, finally concluding:

"Very well. It will be necessary to try cautery. But I warn you that it is a remedy I resort to with soldiers."

The saint shuddered, and then asked:

"When will we try it?"

"As soon as possible, before the poison weakens you too much, for you will need all the strength you can muster."

"Surely the Lord will aid me."

"I hope so." He hesitated for a moment and then came back to her bedside. "There is something, however, that passes my understanding in this case. How will He look upon any attempt to interfere with the workings of His will? It is common knowledge that these wounds are a grace that He has granted to this convent."

My sister remained silent for a moment. Then she answered in a faint, hesitant tone of voice:

"That is quite true. A gift for which we offer thanks each day. I ask only that you remove this pain and that my malady not worsen if your science is capable of bringing such a thing about."

As the doctor replaced her bandages, he shook his head.

"This is an odd way of thinking: making such a clear distinction between the pain and the risk on the one hand, and the miracle on the other; between the corporeal and the supernatural. It would seem that you see very clearly what so many doctors of theology have discussed in vain. It is necessary to accept what the Lord visits upon us, not only insofar as it pleases us but also insofar as it brings us pain. If this were not so, how, for example, could there be martyrs? Even though I for my part prefer, naturally, that you be a saint rather than a dead martyr, and rather than a saint a live woman in good health."

"When, then, shall we try your remedy?"

"Don't worry. I'll send word far enough in advance. God be with you."

"May He be with you."

Since the prioress was in such a state, with high fevers and her body in torment, with agonizing, burning pains in her hands and her mind elsewhere, deeply concerned about the cruel remedy that lay in store, she begged me to take her place as head of the house for a time. The backbiting grew worse once again, since her predecessor deemed that because of her age and rank she should be the one to take over in such a situation; the old woman once again tried to stir up the already troubled waters of the house by bringing to light our long-standing enmity toward her that she had so often punished. All this, along with the recent privileges granted our new guest, her chambermaid and her finery, that immaculate and elegantly furnished cell, were just so many more wounds in her flesh through which melancholy, if not pain at never having known such pleasures herself, crept into her heart, scarcely leaving her time for rest or prayers and spurring her on each day to even more bitter backbiting.

This was the state of affairs in the community when one

morning, around midday, we saw the king's highway come to life again. It was a small cavalry troop. Just as they were about to enter the city, at the very gate, a fair number separated from the rest and came galloping up to within a few feet of our door. The youngest of them all swiftly dismounted.

We all hastened to see what was happening, and were peeking at that fine bunch of dashing cavalrymen from behind the latticed windows when repeated hammerings on the door nearly knocked the house down.

Since the prioress was sick in bed, it fell upon me to receive the newcomers. And so, wondering what had brought them there, what they had come to offer us or more likely what they had come to ask of us, I veiled my face and ordered the portress to open the door. It was out of the question to listen through the turning-box to such an estimable company of gentlemen. I was not mistaken. On our doorstep were four officers whose noble endowments were quite eivdent despite the fatigue of their journey. Our Queen Isabella had said straight out that a bishop conducting a ceremonial rite and a cavalier riding off to war pleased her more than any other sort of men. The sun shone on the trappings of their mounts, on their bits and spurs, straightened their shoulders and tapered their chests.

The three men still on horseback, behind the one who had knocked at the door, seemed like archangels, at once beautiful and terrifying, sent by Our Lord to this humble limbo. When I finally regained my composure and was able to receive them with our usual Ave Maria, the one on foot hastened toward me, sweeping the dust of the entrance with the plume of his hat.

"I never thought, sister, that you nuns in convents were such sound sleepers," he began, whereupon I retorted:

"This is not an hour for sleep but for prayer and work."

"And what task is it that makes you so hard of hearing?"

"A task that with the help of Our Lord is not so hard that it cannot be borne, nor so mean that it does not merit the respect of those who fear Him."

The captain stood there without answering for a moment, scowling and somewhat vexed; but then, in a politer manner and more measured tones, he begged my pardon and informed me of the reason for his visit, which was none other than to speak with our guest.

I knew very well that at court such meetings were allowed and still are even after vows have been taken. I therefore made no objection, since I realized full well that it would no doubt avail me little to do so, but granted my permission only on condition that such a meeting or conversation take place in our locutory, through the grille, and in my presence, as was the rule in such cases.

The captain agreed to everything and acceded to all my conditions, though not without some objection. But then, having been won over by my arguments, he went out to bid his friends goodbye as I went upstairs to announce his arrival to the object of his eagerness and my concern.

On hearing the news I brought, our guest did not seem to be at all excited. Her indifference may have been feigned, or perhaps she had been advised of his arrival beforehand, for with the greatest calm, without the slightest undue haste, she began to dress and adorn herself as though this were an ordinary visit quite within the rules of the house

As her maid hastened to help her, she slowly donned over

her chemise a white bodice and skirt decorated with raised embroidery, cinched at the waist with an embroidered belt. More than a nun, her demeanor and her attire brought to mind a bride about to be wed, a highborn lady on her way to the palace, a queen in ceremonial dress.

Before going downstairs, she wanted to know the name of the person who had asked to see her, and as I apologized for not knowing, she pretended not to know who the visitor was either, and insisted that I reveal his name:

"All he told me was that he is a good friend of yours," I replied.

"Where has he come from?."

"From the court, it would seem."

These last words made her servant all the more eager to finish dressing her mistress. But once she was ready and about to follow me downstairs, she asked me yet another question:

"Does the prioress know?"

"She's still sick in bed in her cell. In any event, I preferred to tell you before I told her. Since the news is bound to reach her sooner or later, you had best hurry."

"You are right, sister," she said, smiling for the first time as we headed for the cloister. "Remind me that I owe you this favor."

Those were her words and her feelings as she peeked through the grille and caught sight of our captain, so eager and so dashing, waiting impatiently. Intuiting immediately that the object of and the reason for his long wait was there in the shadow, he flung himself against the bars, kissing the hands offered to him through them. A beautiful mystery, love, that unites bodies and souls even through such cruel barriers, a sweet poison that leads even its public prosecutors and judges to desire it. I was an accomplice of that meeting, though I never knew whether it was out of eagerness to further the fortunes of the house or out of something close to pleasure at the happy prospect of learning more about the art of love. In any event, seeing the two of them there, intuiting each other's presence, speaking to each other, touching each other as they stood on either side of those bars bristling with studs as sharp as thorns, my heart eagerly followed the words of both, so sweet and so deeply felt, above all in the mouth of the captain, who kept mumbling as though seeking pardon for some recent, secret sin.

As they conversed together, our guest's anger abated. Her words were no longer curt and cutting, and though she no longer sobbed from time to time she had not yet given in entirely. They talked of the war her father was fighting, which was still dragging on; the captain was hastening to join him with his troop of cavalry; she threw it in his face that had such an occasion not arisen, he would never have come to visit her, a reproach her gallant beau countered with protestations of his love, with heated assurances that in her absence no other person or affection had won him over.

Little by little, what with the warmth of their words, they forgot my presence altogether, and the distance to which the grille condemned them as well. Shedding all fear and circumspection, the gallant lover fought to kiss as much of his beloved as he could dimly discern: fingers, eyes, lace, hair, as though she were a talisman or a reliquary sought all the more desperately insofar as it was forbidden to him. No word of caution, no warning seemed capable of curbing his passion, not even the news of the future vows that our new sister would be taking.

"You taking the veil? You a slave?" the captain exclaimed in a half whisper.

"What's so strange about that? It's almost as if you've forgotten what I'm like."

"On the contrary. I say that because I know what you're like. And I shall even go so far as to say that this game of playing convent strikes me as a stupid one."

Our guest's voice grew grave once again:

"I have decided to serve Our Lord God."

"Who could have any objection to that? Each of us does so as befits our station. But yours does not permit you to stay shut up here forever."

"This is my house."

The captain glanced around him.

"A very poor one in my opinion."

"I plan to restore it, with my father's help. To bring it back to life. Soon it will be as famous and attract as many visitors as the other court convents."

"I won't gainsay you that, and I shall not be the one to stand in the way of such plans. I merely came," he added in the same dulcet tones as before, "to assure you that I am as devoted to you as ever."

The captain again approached the grille as though he were about to open it with furtive hands. His face, paler now than before, could barely be seen though the dark latticework of the grille, while his voice sounded even fainter and more dispirited.

"In any event," he insisted, "why not choose another house, a better, more comfortable one? They are all open to you. They all know what a rich dowry you would bring them."

"I have everything I could possible want here."

"There is yet another reason," the captain added in a hesitant tone of voice.

"What reason could be as important as that one?"

"If you went to another house I could visit you frequently. It would not be necessary to wait for another war to take me far from court."

"Vain words," his friend retorted. "Stupid promises. Only a few months ago, how many long days and nights you made me wait—using the same sort of pretexts and excuses!"

"If I failed to come, it was against my will."

"Why not tell the truth?"

"The truth is that the war kept me away, then as now."

Our guest reared back as violently as a mount pricked by a spur.

"That holy and blessed war! Do you think I'm that stupid? Everybody knows all about your wars. Your battles are always fought in beds and bedrooms."

And having delivered herself of that grave accusation, she suddenly turned her back on the visitor. A rustle of silk and the tread of Cordovan leather accompanied her to the door of the locutory which she left wide open behind her as a veiled challenge to the captain, whose sorrowful face was dimly visible in the shadow. The reminder of her wrath was still resounding in the room as her defeated friend retreated with leaden footsteps down the corridor.

A strange destiny, that of these two lovers: turning their backs upon each other in that fashion, hating each other, scorning each other in the best years of their lives, when the pangs of love are most painful, when the wind, the flowers, the birds, the voice of the body, the loneliness of the soul invite lovers to take their pleasure far from grilles and arguments, far from slights and laments. What man ever had before him such attractive company, such ripe passion, reasoning so unreasonable, at once altogether rebellious and altogether submissive! What woman ever proved to be at once so wary and so arrogant, yielding without risking anything, tarrying, fleeing, leaving behind her retreating back a trap laid for the following day!

It was quite evident that our new sister had mastered perfectly that art whereby the soul gives up and surrenders only after a painful battle well fought, wherein the body must never yield at the first invitation but remain ever on guard, even though overcome by love and venal desires.

I was the only one left in the room now, standing alongside the deserted grille, feeling empty inside, sadder than I had thought I would be, hesitating as to whether I ought to go back to my sister and recount what had happened or go ask my new friend for a reward for the favor done her. Unable to decide which course to take, I drew the curtains over the grille and the windows, leaving the locutory in darkness.

I was still pondering that love that had miscarried when a voice, at once quiet and full of fury, reached my ears. I immediately recognized it as being that of the saint, whom the daughter of our protector was answering in her usual arrogant tone. Our guest was upbraiding the prioress for eavesdropping, for having left her bed for that very purpose even though she was ill, with the sole aim of meddling in her affairs, of ordering her about as though she were just another sister when in reality she was the mistress of the house.

"I shall write to my father, and he'll have it closed," she said. "Those famous hands of yours will be incapable of making me change my mind if it suits my fancy to bring about its ruin."

"Lower your voice. Don't you think you've caused enough scandal for one day?"

"What scandal? What new rule is this that gives you the right to decree that visits are forbidden?"

"Only certain visits."

"Is Your Mercy perchance my confesssor?" Who gave you permission to absolve me or punish me?"

The prioress did not answer, but from outside, by straining my ears, I could hear the note of disdain in the voice of the one, speaking from the lofty summit of her pride, and the rancor in the voice of the other, speaking from the less stable height of her recent elevation in the church hierarchy.

"Your Mercy would be well-advised to think before you speak. You had best seclude yourself and meditate, and then we will renew this discussion if it so pleases Your Mercy. But so long as I am here, so long as I am the prioress of this house, please know and do not force me to repeat it yet again, that I have no intention of dealing with this matter by gently cajoling you or allowing you special privileges; I shall go instead to the provincial himself if necessary so that he may take whatever steps he may deem most appropriate."

This said, she left the room more swiftly, surely, than the state of her health and her strength permitted. She went on her way with such rapid steps that she scarcely noticed me. Her billowing mantle brushed aside the honeysuckle on the walls, the casts of dead flies and worms, the plaster dust, the shriveled dead leaves.

And I asked myself what powerful reason had thus brought

her back to life so suddenly, what cause she was defending, what she had gained by openly confronting such a formidable enemy.

Perhaps she had some inkling of the plan that our new sister had in mind: taking over as mistress and head of the house. Perhaps, after her first suspicions had been aroused, she had become convinced that her office was in danger, and who could tell, perhaps her fame as well, attained at such great risk and with such great effort. Then again, it might all well be a game to force our new sister outside the walls, by acceding to her father's request and at the same time obliging her to give up taking vows by being extremely severe with her. It was not difficult then to understand why she had been so eager to rise from her sickbed, why she had listened at the door and then revealed her presence, why her voice was not as steady as it might have appeared to be, and why she took no notice of me as she left, expecting no doubt that I would inform her of everything that had happened, as it was my duty to do.

And what about me? What was I to do, torn in two as I was: on the one hand gazing into my sister's heart, and on the other looking toward future benefits if our new guest's cause prospered?

But truly is it said that Christ loved us, so that if we do not imitate Him, we are not like Him. Neither our acts or our faces are like His; rather, we are poor, blind, and mute, because man lives by love alone. Hence let us love one another, my sister, above and beyond any material comfort or profit, let us love one another and we will be like unto God, let us suffer our anguished loneliness together, let us each suffer in and for the other. I shall not betray you, I shall not sell you, like a latter-day Judas, for the glory of the house, to attain fame and prebends in the shadow of your enemies. Nothing matters to me save you, within me, girded round about my waist with your voice, your breath, your senses. With the two of us as one, let abandonment and disdain come our way in their own good time, for they cannot possibly prevail against us. Let us take our pleasure together, sister, in our bright prison of love, in this sublime shared penitentiary.

The cautery iron is like a tense, cruel arm that, pointing at us, beckons us and then rejects us, leaving us at once racked with pain and relieved of it. Its strongest end, heated as red-hot as a glowing coal, invites and threatens, makes the poor painful flesh of the saint tremble as it rids it of its burning fevers. As it heats on the small camp stove that the doctor has brought with him so as to administer the treatment in her own cell without attracting the attention of the community, it has more the look of an implement of torture, of the sort they say are applied to those accused by the Inquisition, than of a medical instrument to relieve the sufferings of troops wounded in battle.

The doctor turns it round and round on the bed of hot coals to heat it to precisely the right temperature, as my sister meanwhile prays at his back, on her knees alongside her bed that has been readied to receive her, doing her best to pluck up her courage in the face of the frightening prospect before her, asking the Lord to give her the strength to endure this trial if He is still willing to bestow His grace upon her. None of the three of us speak or exchange glances or hearken to anything save the pounding of our hearts and the loud sizzling of the coals. From outside the only sound to be heard is the call of the swifts and from time to time some echo or other from the city that in the early morning silence seems to glide effortlessly across the expanse of cultivated fields.

The king's highway is alive with the pounding of hoofs, the creak of carts, prolonged whinnies. Within these blessed walls of ours, on the other hand, it would seem that everyone has fallen silent: in the garden, the choir, the kitchen, and the workroom where the novices weave their panniers and little rush baskets. No one murmurs or laughs, there is no sound of voices, it is as though even the restless swallows and the black crows are waiting motionless. It is as though, like the three of us there in the cell, they have fallen silent, some of them out of fear of their own fear and others out of pity for the pain that those frightful hands are about to suffer.

Suddenly, lost in thought, I hear the voice of the doctor standing next to the little stove, announcing that the instrument is ready. It is true. It is lying there waiting alongside him, red-hot, almost white. My sister has finally risen from her knees, turned toward him, and is looking at him in fear and trembling. In a weak, quavering voice, she murmurs:

"Couldn't we wait just a little while more?"

"Set you mind at rest. We have the entire day before us to do what must be done."

The doctor, it is plain to see, is eager to make light of the task that lies before him, but there is no point in avoiding inflicting pain when the need for it has proved to be inevitable. Moreover, the entire house would be altered were the operation to be postponed. What purpose would be served by retreating if the poison is there, plain to see, black, gnawing, oozing? Better to attack than to wait for it to grow and spread uncontrollably.

The doctor too has fallen silent as he follows his own train of thought. From time to time he fans the coals and the blast of air from the bellows makes one's flesh shudder, and our eyes are thereby drawn to the hands now free of their bandages. They are in full view now: as dirty and dark as the mud in the bottom of the well, like wheat fields in autumn, broken, ragged, strewn with clods.

When my sister saw herself with bare arms and hands, with the sleeves of her habit rolled up, exposing as much flesh as the rule permits in such cases, she again felt unsteady on her feet and it was necessary to hold her up to keep her from collapsing on the floor. Taking her in my arms, I fought to revive her, to try to communicate to her something of my courage; though scant and feeble, it was nonetheless full of love, and I would willingly have suffered her terrible pain in her place. She turned her eyes toward me on feeling me so close and yielded to my entreaties, allowing me to seat her in a chair especially readied for her. The our doctor took a thin wooden rod from his valise and placed it between her teeth.

"When the pain gets bad, it is best to bite down on it. It will help."

And without giving her any more time to procrastinate, he bound her arms to those of the chair, so swiftly and surely that almost without her noticing, the saint's hands and feet were now immobilized, awaiting their enemy that was now approaching, lighting the air with its white glow as it came toward her.

"Lord in Heaven, what must the flames of Hell be like!"

179

the saint murmured, bathed in sweat and averting her eyes brimming with tears.

"I warned you that it was a cruel remedy."

"Won't they discover what you've done tomorrow?"

"Set your mind at rest, sister. No one will know a thing. I shall make a bandage even stouter than the one you had before."

I stepped away from the two of them for a moment and carefully opened the door. There wasn't a soul to be seen outside. The only sound was the quiet flow of the water in the hidden conduits of the irrigation ditch. A strong gust of autumn wind suddenly shook the stocks of the grapevines, the dark shadows of the ivy, but finally everything was quiet and peaceful once again. There was no sign of life, nothing stirred save my wildly pounding heart, which once I went back inside the cell began to beat faster still when I saw the red-hot iron tongue in the doctor's hands, moving toward its victim.

In an instant the entire cell was filled with the smell of charred flesh, with a shout muffled by a gag. My sister appeared to be about to burst her bonds, but in the end all her strength abandoned her and her head that had toppled over onto her chest indicated to us that she could no longer see or feel anything. I tried to raise it up, not to enable her to contemplate the doctor standing waiting next to the coals, but to support it in my lap as the tongue of fire came her way once again, white and terrible.

The doctor was coming back with the searing-iron held on high; then he thrust it out before him, angled it downward and applied it. Again there was that same stench, along with a dry, muffled hiss that seemed to pierce to the very bone.

He must have long been accustomed to manipulating the iron, for he barely touched it to her skin, as though trying to avoid hurting her more than necessary. Afterward he examined the mark it had left and extinguished the iron in a bowl of water. It had left two horrible holes like the mouth of Hell, and that smell that, without my being able to say why, brought death to mind more forcefully than the graves in our cemetery. Then it was necessary to bandage her again, to put her back in bed, and wait till the doctor left so as to undress her, very gently. The doctor, for his part, declared that if the cure depended on medical science alone, her hands would be well within a month, and then, having picked up his instrument, he finally left, dismissing me with his usual brusque gesture when I offered to escort him out.

"She needs you more. Try to get her to rest. It is necessary to help nature along."

What can my sister have seen in her dreams? With whom could she have been speaking aloud? Whom was she addressing when she tossed and turned between the sheets? Entire nights moaning, crying out in a low voice, wounded—I never knew why or by whom, nor whether it was her spirit or her hands that had been wounded.

At times she called out to her father, that wretched little man, thin and olive-skinned, who had appeared at the house one day, tugging her along by the hand. A man who spoke like a gentleman but who came on foot, with no other retinue save a few relatives covered with mud, brutish and silent.

By their gaze, at once haughty and beaten, guarded and hostile, it was plain to see that they were gentry who had lost rank and fortune, no doubt ruined like so many others by the calamities of recent years. They obviously had grave doubts about leaving the girl with us, despite the father's assurances as to her vocation. A sad desire, a lamentable vocation, as could be seen from her threadbare wardrobe, skirts and bodices that between them had seen as many years and as many leagues of wear and tear as the battered road that had brought them there.

More than gentlefolk, they had the look of the poorest and most dispirited peons, of those who see only coarse rye bread, fried crumbs, and meat of animals that have died a natural death, of those who go about stuffed like sausages into quilted jackets and fur pelts that ill disguise long involuntary fasts, abandoned property, and days wasted in useless lawsuits.

Surely it was to them that my sister shouted in her dreams, perhaps fleeing from the memory of them on seeing them standing there at her very bedside. Perhaps her mother stepped forward, kissed her as she had done on that day long ago, and knelt before her, hoping for her blessing like those who today flocked to the house in droves from outside the walls, fighting for a bit of her hair, for a bloody little strip of cloth.

But the saint's words were addressed neither to her nor to the wretched little man. Many nights, as I watched over her, I tried my best to discover the reason for her outcries. As soon as I had closed the door so that the sound of her shouting would not be heard in the passageway outside, I tried to make out some recognizable name amid the chaos of her ravings, but her voice always fell silent too soon and I knew no more than I had before.

On those nights as the seasons changed, I never contrived to learn who her enemy was; other sisters may have had better luck than I, but for my part, my hours with her were fruitless as winter gave warning signs of its approach, sweeping the plain with its curtains of gorse and thistle. It finally came with its brief light so wan and weary that it saddened one's soul and made me weep over my sister's body, that body so lush and soft once upon a time and today emaciated and in pain, abandoned by everyone save me, as I now paid back her love with charity, her silences of the past with renewed pleasure at being there in the cell with her, far from the world both within and without the house.

In the beginning, in the first days, a few sisters had appeared at the door.

"Is the prioress up and about?"

"Has she come out of her stupor?"

"We hear tell that her wounds have disappeared recently. May the Lord forbid that this be so!"

"He surely would not do anything to our detriment."

I merely nodded, pointing at her hands whose bandages I changed every day, and reassured, they went off satisfied, seemingly more interested in the benefits of the miracle than in the health of the saint that they were asking after.

The guest of the house also came to visit us. As usual, she entered without warning or hesitation, followed by her ever-present maidservant. From her hauteur, which she never abandoned, her gaze swept round the cell, examining the cracked walls, the wretched furniture, the bare floor so different from hers. Then she lowered her eyes and scrutinized us in silence. Seeing her standing there appraising us, weighing us, my sister especially, one would think that it was she, not the saint, who was the prioress.

"Is she sleeping?" she asked me.

"She's resting at least."

"How long has she been like this?" Just as I was about to answer, she interrupted me in her usual manner: "How long has it been since the doctor has seen her?"

"Don't worry, we're expecting him."

"When?"

"One of these days. He recommended that we be patient till then."

"A remedy that doctors greatly favor. Unfortunately it cures only certain ills. If the one she is suffering from gets no better and we continue to have no one to govern the house, it will be necessary to hold another election, because as the Holy Book says, it is not good for a flock to be without a shepherd, for the sheep will scatter and be lost."

I did not answer, but as she was leaving, she added:

"Those wounds may well come to nothing and even be used against her if they come to the attention of the Holy Office."

She left the cell with her shadow following along behind her, leaving me full of remorse and deeply concerned, remembering her tone of voice, fearing that she would intervene to put an end to our fraud, which now involved not only the peace of the house but also the risk of prison, the twin fruits of one and the same garden.

Perhaps she was not as stupid as the other sisters, nor as

mercenary. After all, she came from the court, not from the countryside with its petticoats and wooden clogs, far from other richer and more important places. Perhaps she was able to distinguish between the things of this world and the wonders of the world beyond, between the Lord's gifts and those miracles without heaven's help that are meant to fulfill humble dreams.

It was she who must have been responsible for that ill-fated reversal of our fortunes that began just as the saint's condition was improving, when her reason was returning, when she was again able to recognize my voice, when her eyes lit up once again on hearing me.

The blood began to flow in her vitals once more and except for not yet being able to stand up, she seemed so well and strong that we were awaiting only the doctor's permission to take her out into the cloister. Then one morning I came upon our guest deep in conversation with the chaplain. Both of them had grave, worried expressions on their faces. I didn't hear what they were saying, but when I told my sister of this, I saw that she was no longer in the same good spirits as in recent days.

"What's the trouble? Has your fever come back again? We mustn't let the doctor think we're lazybones," I said, trying to cheer her up.

But despite my words, her strength of the days just past was flagging. I was obliged to put her back to bed again.

"After being completely prostrated for so many days, it's not surprising that you tire easily."

"Was I in such a sorry state as that?"

"Yes, at times."

"Did I say anything I shouldn't have at such times?"

"Not a single word that anyone could hear as long as I was here at your side."

"Who else kept watch over me?"

"A number of the sisters, according to the schedule we set up. Even the old prioress spent many an afternoon in the cell. What matters most now, however, is that you don't have a fever."

"Did the doctor come too?" she asked, unwilling to drop the subject.

"The one thing he recommended was rest. And you can see now how right he was to choose the remedy he did."

Shortly thereafter, as though in answer to her questions and my doubts, the little bell announcing the doctor's visit sounded in the passageway.

We barely had time to veil our faces before he entered the cell without waiting for our greeting. His tone of voice was very different now than when he had been speaking with the chaplain, and his manner and movements more self-assured and gentle as he confirmed the improvement in the saint's condition, which in his opinion marked the beginning of a complete recovery.

He seemed very interested on learning that the invalid had been on her feet again, so much so that his visit did not last even half as long as the previous onces. He promised to come back later and went to compare his opinion with that of the chaplain, who had just come into the cell and was walking over to her bedside, more eager to hear her confession than to look after the health of her body.

"Is it true that you're beginning to feel well again?"

"Why are you asking me that again?"

"Because we heard and saw Your Mercy in states such that we asked ourselves whether you might not have permanently lost your senses."

"On the contrary. I have never been more in possession of my senses than at this moment. But be that as it may: what is it you want of me?"

The chaplain fell silent. He stepped away from the bed and glanced up at the crucifix as though awaiting help, or perhaps an answer. Then he looked in the direction of the half-open door and finally, with a sigh, began speaking:

"To our misfortune our house has fallen upon fateful days."

"Fateful? I've never seen better ones."

"I for my part have seen better ones, and it is for that reason that I can attest to the truth of what I say. This house has been in an uproar ever since you fell ill. Even your guest seems ill-disposed toward us. She is talking of leaving us."

"And why should her petty annoyances be of any concern to me? She may leave whenever she pleases."

"And thereby cause the house to lose her father's favor?"

"We were over the worst before she came. Why shouldn't we prosper now?"

The chaplain fell silent once more; once again the sound of his footsteps measured off the silence in the cell.

"In any event, that it not the principal reason for my visit," he stated, in an even graver tone of voice. "I have come above all else so as to be able to report on the state of your health."

"My health? And to whom are you to report on it?"

"To someone outside the house."

"And to whom can my state of health be of any interest?"

Another silence, then his voice as clear as the light of day, as quiet as a dart winging through the air.

"To the Holy Office. I recently received a denunciation of the two of you," he said, including both of us in one sweeping gesture, and then added: "The Holy Office is not in the habit of revealing who called upon it or why."

"I am well aware of that without your having to tell me. That denunciation surely came from someone in this house."

"In view of your illness, we have been ordered to keep you under lock and hey here, confined to your cell. As soon as witnesses can be called the usual trial will take place."

"Will it be some time yet before it begins?"

"Be patient and pray to the Lord. Don't lose hope. He always saves those who trust in Him. If it is true that they have sinned, there is no more merciful judge."

Vain words, stupid arguments. Just as I had feared, the hand of fate was descending swiftly upon us. The moment the chaplain left I took refuge in the saint's arms. For the first time since we had put our plan in motion, I felt her tremble, and for good reason. The mere mention of the Holy Office made one's courage falter.

"Sister, they're going to burn both of us at the stake for our sins."

"Don't be afraid," she answered, trying to raise my spirits. "Though our sin is grave, forgiveness is infinite."

"Not that of men."

"Even in this world there must be just powers."

Perhaps it was because of her sickness, but once she had lost her fear, it was she who took it upon herself to lie, trying to cheer me, to banish my tears.

We knew full well the steps that would be taken as soon as the doctor decreed that her illness was ended, that the saint had regained her health.

188

To our misfortune our respite was a very brief one, and before a week was out, he was back, accompanied by two familiars of the Holy Office. Without respect for my sister's state of health, after closely questioning the former prioress and the other sisters, they set a date when we would be obliged to leave the convent and go with them. Our protests and arguments were in vain—to the great satisfaction of some, the former prioress above all, our guest, and a small group who had soon rallied round her, and to the even greater dismay of the others who accused the Holy Tribunal of lending a willing ear to anonymous denunciations.

Very shortly, in the space of a few hours, that apparent calm of previous days, that silence charged with passions and bitterness seemed to explode like a mine with a lighted fuse. The entire house, from the gate to the choir, was rife with awesome hatreds and constant rancors. Our Lord's sword seemed to divide the community in two: on the one hand, there were those who still regarded the new prioress as a saint, and on the other, those who in a matter of days dared to accuse her of being a fraud. Thus everything was thrown into chaos: prayers, work, visits, meals. Even sleep was forgone as the sisters took sides for or against, attending one or another of the conclaves that took place each night in various cells to discuss the matter till the break of dawn. It was no longer a question of her wounds, which appeared to have been swept aside, forgotten. In their eagerness to save her, the partisans who had suddenly rallied to her cause discovered new prodigies now to feed into the mill of her fame, which once they were bruited about outside the walls, increased and multiplied.

Such stories had that the Virgin and the saints frequently

visited her. Even the Holy Child descended one night to comfort her, leaving her as a memento of His visit a thorn from his crown on the Mount of Calvary imbedded in her temple. Her supporters swore she took no nourishment other than the Holy Eucharist, which was capable of rescuing from hell an infinite number of souls, saving more than a hundred at a time. And what was more, her ardent defenders went back to the long-ago days of her childhood, roundly asserting that even as a little girl, by merely laying her hands on the sick, she had caused them to recover their health, like latter-day Lazaruses resurrected from the grave.

Rumors of such wonders even reached the ears of her parents, and the news of their hasty return to the convent, their eagerness to testify to such marvels, swearing wholeheartedly that even as a child my sister had performed such miracles, spread far and wide.

There they were, awaiting the end of her adventure with no thought for anything save their own interests, without the least concern for the more and more uncertain and precarious fate confronting the saint.

Dressed in their garments of long ago, that might well have been taken out of the family chest for the occasion after having been carefully stored away ever since the day their daughter had first taken her vows, they came to the gate very early every morning, sought permission to visit her, which usually the portress refused to grant them, and returned to the city, battered in body and soul but still not admitting defeat.

Our guest meanwhile did not let a single moment or opportunity go by to ruin the saint's reputation, pointing out in no uncertain terms—and perhaps it was true—that as far as stigmata and wounds were concerned, they were so widely sown throughout the country that they could be harvested as readily as wheat in summer, filling the granaries of the entire kingdom. Mystic ecstasies and saintly raptures were so common that it was the rare convent that did not pride itself on its own particular miracle, and even laymen and pious women laid claim to them, the latter especially, inasmuch as their sex is weaker in the head, has more vivid imaginations than men, takes the illusions of the Devil to be signs from God, and is incapable of distinguishing between matters of the soul and corporeal phenomena.

There was such violent contention between the two sides that rumors of their clashes leapt over our convent walls and reached the city. Then the rumor spread that they were trying to remove the prioress from the house, and an angry mob set up camp outside the gate. It was quite something to hear the storm, the hurricane of voices that from daybreak on echoed through the cells and the patios, wailing at times and at others threatening, beseeching that she not be allowed to leave, vowing to take the matter to the provincial of our order, to the king our sovereign.

The church was filled with faces that barely followed the mass, the words of the priest, so frequently did they turn their eyes toward the grille, trying their best to make out, beyond the bars, those white bandaged arms they remembered so well, a guarantee of salvation that they were about to lose forever. In vain the chaplain sought their attention, endeavored to calm those present with promises of her immediate return. Lacking both composure and devotion, that mob could only sob, moan, and at times utter insulting remarks under their breath in protest against the Holy Tribunal and its secret procedures.

And then yet another plague descended upon us in the few days that remained before our departure. This one came in the form of crosses, medals, and relics that invaded the esplanade in front of our entrance—hawked, sold, venerated, the vestiges perhaps of other past devotions, though now a great flock of false pilgrims loudly claimed that those objects had touched the hands and garments of the saint. Men and women of every rank and age fought over those bits of cloth, those locks of hair, those pieces of paper with writing on them, some of them paying whatever sum was asked for them, and others pleading and even resorting to violence to get their hands on them.

What was even more remarkable was my sister's silence when she heard from my lips the news of these throes of ecstatic passion.

"Let the rumor of those miracles spread, sister," she said to me. "They will favor our cause when we appear before the judges."

"But we both know that they are false."

"How do we know what is false and what is not? What do we know of human nature? What is true today is no longer so tomorrow. A person alive today has no way of knowing if he will live to see the morrow. Life, sister, is like a river that cannot be contained. We have the impression that we are diverting it, controlling it, using it as we please, but it flows on, and no force in heaven or on earth is capable of making it run backward, halt, or die. It is the same with us humans. Only the Lord in His infinite wisdom is able to judge or to condemn; our destiny lies in His hands alone."

"But we have both lied," I insisted, lost in the midst of

these vague ramblings. "From the very first, we have never told the truth. And we still haven't."

"There is no one in this world capable of judging us."

Mayhap her illness, her dreams, had disturbed her reason, erasing from her memory our initial deception, the first consequences of which we were now suffering. Or else everything was an illusion, a figment of my imagination; perhaps it was my reason, my memory, that had given way and were not functioning properly. Mayhap those two dark stains, so turbid and fetid beneath the red-hot tongue of the searing-iron were merely something that I had dreamed, not something that had been the work of my hand, cut into her flesh vein by vein. Perhaps in my sister's eyes no risk confronted her, since she would be obliged to prostrate herself only before our eternal, natural judge. But I for my part felt myself in mortal peril, and I could already see myself before that awesome earthly tribunal, with its terrifying judges and its ways of wresting the truth as it had from so many other heretics, frauds, and apostates. What was to become of me if my sister and my Lord abandoned me? Would I be able to hide the truth, or would I ruin her good name and damn both myself and her?

193

Chapter Six

W E made our way toward the city where the Tribunal was to examine us. We had not made a whirlwind departure from the convent, amid thundering hoofs and loud shouts. Women had tried to block the path; men, being stronger, had done their best to pull my sister out from the coach; cripples wailed and people from the city crossed themselves in silence, muttering prayers. Our guards fought to keep the road cleared, but the multitude at times threatened to surround us, to make us turn back, to seek refuge inside the walls that we were leaving behind. From the town opposite, from many other villages and settlements such a great crowd gathered that as it took over the entire plain, the scene became more reminiscent of a Last Judgment than of a devout farewell.

The sun was as red as usual in that season, and someone, on seeing how roughly the saint was being treated, began to murmur that it was bleeding like her wounds. A universal weeping and wailing arose among her devoted followers and soon turned into a chorus of angry shouts on both sides of the bars. There inside the house, behind the latticed windows, we could sense the grief of certain sisters and the silent rejoicing of others, the prelude to the war that was about to break out behind us once our coach departed.

We would never have managed to go on had it not been for the constables and a spearhead of cavalrymen who, by making a sally, scared off the most fainthearted and kept at bay the most determined, leaving them badly frightened or battered and bruised. What happened next was not what they had anticipated, however, for the crowd that had again formed after the charge kept following us and singing the saint's praises, fighting to touch even the wheels of the coach or the wood of the bodywork. The saint peeked out every so often, despite her guards, and it was something to see how the multitude again crowded in closer, in greater and greater numbers, obliging us to slow down to match the pace of the most aged among them.

Sitting opposite my sister, peering beyond the curtains, I was terror-stricken to see how our lie had now been compounded by scandal, and asked myself whether her spirit still dwelt within her mortal flesh or whether, having been carried away by her illness, it was now journeying along the path to eternal madness.

Perhaps in her pride, having completely forgotten our first days in the house, she was now living the happiest moments of her life, there amid those who acclaimed her as we passed, showering her with praise, commending their children, their maladies, their lives to her. Perhaps glory was hers for a day, for a few hours, amid the din that reached our ears from outside, amid the tumult of voices, amid that agitated sea of fame, untroubled by a single thought of me, of her parents whom she had not even bothered to bid goodbye, of the old prioress, of our guest who in recent days had scarcely shown her face, of the entire house to which mayhap neither of the two of us would ever return.

Now the sea is not following us but preceding us. From the next town, a league away, yet another tempest approaches, which soon joins the one that has engulfed us. Even before we are able to make out anything save its belltower, it seems plain that the entire town has turned out, and bearing crosses and banners, is slowly coming to join us. Finally the two groups meet and become one. The people look the same, though these newcomers are less weary, more stubborn, and determined. Our fame is growing more than even my sister ever dreamed it would. Hence this journey, rather than frightening her, is causing her to swell with pride, strengthening her, reassuring her. Though it is still as though we are blind, able to see only what the curtains of the coach allow us to, it is quite evident that the sea surrounding us is rising and becoming stormier, the sound of it growing more muffled as we proceed down the main street and the hoofs of the mules and voices echo down it.

At times I look, beyond my veil, at the guard escorting us. He in turn looks away toward the taffeta shade protecting us from the sun and the dust. His sullen expression turns to one of concern. His manner suggests that he would like to step up the pace of the animals pulling the coach.

At each village we pass through, he must fear that the crowds are going to stop the team, take the carriage by storm, and drag the two of us off—to jail or to the church altars, I am not certain which. Hence we go straight on without stopping to eat or to quench our thirst, without a halt to satisfy our common bodily needs. We are thirsty, or at least I am, as I ride along half curious and half terrified, with no notion of what part of the country we are crossing, or of the fate that awaits us at the end of such a hasty journey. We are flying through the air, carried along without touching the ground by the faith of a multitude capable of razing towns and setting mountains on fire, of following us for a long time on its knees, of kissing the hoofprints left in the road, and fighting to reach the footboards of the coach at the risk of being crushed to death beneath the wheels.

Each time that voices are raised in prayer round about us, that some tumultuous impromptu chorus attempts to sing a hymn in tune, I wonder what would become of us if those who are honoring and accompanying us today discovered the truth, if they came to learn how and when the whole story began. Perhaps what our guest said is true, that it is a rare convent that does not have its stigmata or miraculous visions or blessed nuns, but these people must be in great need to have followed after us as they have, at the cost of such sacrifices. They must have great faith, many unsatisfied hopes, vast misery of body and soul to thus refuse to let their saint be taken from them, to thus honor and serve her insofar as our guards will permit or the Holy Tribunal allow. Poor people, swept along like this, confident victims of two wicked women, the one moved by a pride disguised as devotion, the other dragged along out of blind love, capable of accompanying her to the very stairs leading to the stake.

May God remove such a vision from my sight. The two of

us facing each other, on our thrones of wood and straw, about to be set on fire by the tinder. Who can say if the flames of this world burn more gently than those others of eternity on this already badly abused flesh, sated one day with passion and starved now of all love? What can the absence of the Lord be like compared to this absence? How can His eternity be compared with this endless rocking to and fro in the swaying coach, lifted to the clouds by the din of voices and the songs that reach our ears from the outside? What a miracle the love that thus remains and endures, with scant nourishment, enjoyed in silence, the key that locks the gate against all evil and makes us seek refuge in the few short years when memory flourishes! There the two of us will be, face to face on the solemn platform. Or perhaps side by side. Rather that, for then, as in life, the same fire will consume us. It will rise upward from your feet, climb up your flesh, to your hands, along the path traced so many times by my hands. The same fire will come to unite us at that moment, just as in the past, and in like fashion it will cause us to lose our senses and our reason, to die, to sink down and down together, leaving the two of us forever one at last.

As midday approached we stopped for a meal, since in the midst of our stormy departure no one had remembered to serve us a single mouthful that morning. Our carriage halted and with it the multitude following us, crowding about to see the saint climb down. She had barely set foot on the ground when the long-suffering flock of the faithful flung itself bodily upon her, fighting to tear away just one little piece of her habit or her mantle or to touch to her feet some of the relics that they had brought with them. In vain the constable ordered them to disperse. Like a sea of grain in summer, those heads drifted back, until we finally reached the entrance and swiftly crossed the patio. There is the room that had been set aside for us amid old reed screens, a table, and two worm-eaten chairs, sitting in front of plates with leftover stew, a little cheese and some raisins, we endeavored to stave off the hunger that had been stalking us since early that morning. With its stout bars over the windows, the room looked more like a prison cell, closed up and dark, lighted only by a gloomy oil lamp.

We sat there facing each other, not knowing what to say, with no great desire to break our day's fast, as if, once we were alone, we suddenly had more than our fill of food and silence. Though there were no eyes watching us, I again found her as aloof, as distant as she had been all during these last days, indifferent even to the fearful days that no doubt were soon to come.

I on the other hand, wept inwardly as I thought of the punishment, of what it was going to be like for my relatives to receive such news. Remembering them, realizing what a blow it would be to them if the Tribunal found us guilty as I feared it would, I would readily have burst into sighs, but my sister's silence both frightened me and made me contain myself. And hence I finally merely murmured:

"Misfortune awaits us, sister."

"Don't be afraid," she answered. "They can't do anything to us. No one is capable of thwarting the designs of Him who watches over us."

"And how do you know that He will come to our aid?"

"Because the Lord helps those who believe in Him simply and wholeheartedly."

"And is that how Your Mercy loves Him?"

"In precisely that way. Any attempt on the part of my enemies to harm me will be of no avail. My answer is to deliver myself over body and soul to His goodness. He will do the rest. He will know how to fight for me, as my spouse and my friend."

Such words were new to me. I could scarcely follow her meaning, but from what I gathered, it seemed clear to me that the Lord, or to put it another way, her pride was blinding her more and more with each passing day as she mounted one by one the steps that might well lead her to the stake.

"What does the soul amount to unless it is in torment?" she went on. "Like the body, it is mere clay. A life without risk is worth very little. In order to lift ourselves above the earth it is necessary to suffer every sort of mortification here below. What does the fire of the stake matter if another fire, that of love, sets the soul aflame and consumes it?"

As far as love was concerned, all I knew was the heat of that other fire that had united us in the past. Of what concern were humiliation and contempt to me? In what way was the Lord honored by such privations? Such humiliation as hers was born of her secret vanity that waxed by the day as the destiny that awaited us drew closer and closer. In my eyes that triumph that she so loudly proclaimed did not appear to be one, no doubt because the Lord does not give all of us the same light of understanding, yet my powers of reason were nonetheless sufficient to illuminate the path that her unreason was taking, a path that step by step was leading her away from me.

"My pleasure lies in becoming one with the Lord," she

assured me, and I, to my woe, felt the painful pangs of jealousy, along with a cruel loneliness that at times counseled me to flee, to abandon her in this new labyrinth into which she had ventured.

"And what about hell? And death? Does Your Mercy not fear them either?"

She looked at me in silence, and finally replied:

"In death there lies true life, the greatest wisdom, forgiveness of our most grievous sins, the surest path to heaven."

I was hard put to understand these new thoughts of hers. They seemed to me to be mere pretenses to justify her abandoning me, now that having been placed upon her pedestal she neither feared me nor needed me. I was scarcely impressed by her new arrogance, that new wisdom that sounded so strange to my ears, absorbed who knew where, learned from who knew what pages.

And so I lowered my eyes, agreeing in silence with her arguments, trying to appease my gnawing hunger, wherein she imitated me, till our stewpot was as empty as my heart was full of questions.

Another night is now descending from the mountaintops, a night that promises to be cruel, for as it falls it brings us ever closer to the day when we shall be obliged to wage common battle against fear. The fields are silent beneath the chill breeze that is beginning to stir the furze, our mantles, our rough lap rugs. Those following us are silent, numb with cold, with aching feet, though their devotion still withstands the gusts of wind and the fatigue of an entire day of trailing after the carriages. Their faith can be divined in the sound of their footfalls, in the murmur of voices when someone, unable to remain on his feet, collapses, his head in the dust, or leaves the road and falls amid the brush alongside the members of his family. From time to time there reaches our ears from the other side of the curtains a clamor of tumultuous voices, angrily urging the others to step up the pace, even cursing them, but soon the voices die down, give up, become once again a monotonous chorus, in time to the rhythm of the footsteps slowly beginning to follow us once again.

No one is capable of stopping our procession, neither the cavalry escort that keeps mercilessly harrying the crowd without knowing why, nor the sun of this new day that again overpowers the weakest, nor this strong wind that takes the oldsters' breath away when night falls. All of them keep following after the saint, singing, praying, recounting wondrous miracles. Doubtless no one is listening to anyone else, but as though each of them is ready and willing to confront a personal enemy, their own shouts and protests give all alike the courage to go on, uplifting their hearts. Such is the faith that must sustain them, quite different, surely, from that which the saint preaches in her solitude. This must be the faith that is said to move mountains, as it impels this mountain of shadows round about us onward.

Our faithful flock falls silent now; all of us—pilgrims, soldiers, guards—make not a single sound. My sister has closed her eyes and is sleeping or pretending to sleep. Who can tell? perhaps fear is building its nest within her. Mayhap in the depths of her heart she too is counting the days that remain. Perhaps she is weeping for her fate, though not for mine;

perhaps she is trembling in the night. When all is said and done, her fate is still undecided. They bless her as a saint now, but it is the Lord who will say whether we will end our days like so many others, shut up behind walls, dead while yet alive, remembered only in prayers and on medals sold in the markets amid cabbages and oil and baskets of nuts.

But very soon such presentiments vanish as though swept away by the wind. A bell rings out far in the distance, and we know very well what its voice is saying. Another town, another village is welcoming us. My sister opens her eyes and sighs.

"Are we reaching the end of our journey?"

And then, listening to the sound of the bronze bell, she realizes, as I do, that this is only another little hamlet.

"May the Lord grant that we find lodgings."

"The guards will know where to find them."

We do our best to see past the curtain but it is still pitch black out and by the gleam of a faint light that comes and goes far in the distance, we can just barely make out the same silhouettes that accompany us by day. They step up the pace now, sensing the presence of others coming to meet them.

Again they found us a large chamber in ruins. Rather than being invited into it, we were locked inside it, as though two women, alone and without money, after a day such as the one we had had, were capable of choosing between taking off and staying for at least a night's rest. And yet my heart kept urging me to flee, leading me to see very clearly the danger that would confront the two of us as soon as our journey came to an end.

My eyes kept glancing all around, but my sister seemed calm. Seeing her sitting there like that, her mind at rest, I asked myself what would become of me if she were some day taken from me, and I was still searching for the answer when from outside the door there came the sound of voices, among which I recognized those of our guards.

They were speaking of us as though we were criminals. One of them asked if it wouldn't be better to wait till after dark to enter the city, thus avoiding any sort of commotion; someone else answered that there was no reason to go about things in such a way, as though the Tribunal found it necessary to hide its trials from the light of day. Despite much discussion, they never came to an agreement, or rather, they put off a decision until the arrival of a courier from the city who was to come to meet us at dawn.

All of them were exhausted and went off to get some sleep, some of them in the chamber opposite ours, and others in one or another of the many garrets of the house. Only the two of us were left awake despite our bone-deep fatigue, till the stars highest in the sky faded and sleep overcame us, the two of us lying together on the same bed, as we had in times past.

Once we were on our way again, we experienced the same sort of morning as before, with more songs and conversations all around us, with the same hills in the distance from which, once the fog had lifted, we saw new throngs of the devout arriving. The cultivated fields and gardens told us that the city was not far off, as did the golden threshing floors and the adobe walls, the greater zeal of the troop of cavalry, and the multitude of carts that by now were accompanying us. New lines of them coming down different neighboring roads suddenly converged, their wheels creaking, their ponderous silhouettes moving slowly through the dust. Mules, people on foot, horses, and men-at-arms milled about, as though ready to do battle. The newcomers had now met up with the army opposite; the two merged, grouped around our coach, destroying irrigation ditches and sowed fields as they passed. A sound of many voices reaching across the entire plain grew louder as the morning light grew brighter, a chorus repeated without rhythm or harmony, by as many echoes as there were villages, as many voices as there were towers and belfries. Dogs and birds alike fell silent now, terrified by that prolonged song, not one of joy as my sister supposed, but, rather, one of foreboding, of secret fears.

For a moment the cavalry troop was obliged to intervene by making a sortie that knocked to the ground those who had advanced farthest, opening a path for us for a short time. Once the road was clear, we managed to make out the bank of the river and the bridge leading across the stream to the city. I fancied that the cross of the roadside shrine was our cross, and a lonely open field the color of straw the place where the autos-da-fe must be held. No one so informed me, no one pointed that dreary, cruel, deserted plot of ground out to me, but my heart told me that that was the spot by pounding even harder as we crossed the river and approached the great city gate that looked to my eyes like the entrance to the antechamber of hell.

And yet, inside the city, what jubilation, what a pealing of bells, what crowds waiting in the streets, and peering out the windows, what clusters of faces perched on balconies, as on the occasion of royal baptisms or weddings.

I never knew whether they were expecting to see us freed or burned at the stake, if our life or death would be in their eyes a warning from heaven or a sign of redemption. My sister, suddenly disturbed, sat there without a word, not daring to look beyond the curtains, and for the first time during the journey, I saw her tremble, hiding her hands beneath her mantle.

I did not want to see any more, and placing our fate in the Lord's hands, I closed my eyes too, allowing my ears to become the couriers of what was happening outside. The bells, the voices set up such a discordant jangle that it was useless to listen. We must have proceeded a fair distance in that fashion, rocked to and fro by the jostling amid the shouts of the crowd, till the coach finally halted and was suddenly flooded with light as a sign from our guards that we were to get out.

Single combat, open battle again became the order of the day as the faithful tried to discover which of the two of us was the saint. Eyes and hands sought us out, searched us, poked and pried till they found the bandaged hands. The mob went wild then, fighting to touch the saint's mantle, ripping off her veil, struggling to kiss her sandals.

Even in her dreams of glory, surely, she had never expected such frenzy, such tumultuous fame. Once again it was necessary to clear a path for us, until after much pushing and shoving, with our feet barely touching the ground at times, we finally reached the entrance of what was henceforth to be our lodgings and our jail and, to my misfortune, the beginning of our permanent separation.

We bade each other farewell there at the very entrance, and for the first time in the months just past our strength dissolved in tears and a trembling from head to foot as though our very life itself were ebbing away. For a moment I could still hear her footsteps as she disappeared down a corridor, and then I was suddenly shoved into a cell no larger than the one I had occupied back in the convent.

Little by little, in the dreary darkness there loomed up before me a wooden platform with a straw mattress, two small jars, one containing a little water and the other, as I soon guessed, intended to be used for various bodily necessities, the entire cell shut off, surrounded by impenetrable loneliness, its one opening to the outside world a tiny little window sealed off by a double grille.

And where had they taken my sister? To what end would the accusation hanging over our heads lead her? Would she be defeated, overwhelmed as I was, or valiant, firm in her faith, sure of herself, and certain of the help of heaven?

When all was said and done, innocent or not, she had arrived there like a queen. As for myself on the other hand, no one paid the least attention to me. I seemed, rather, to be her maidservant—until such time at least as they came to take my deposition. She was the mistress; in the world's eyes I was dust, nothing, not even her shadow.

Once our two sisters were taken off to their prison cells, the one who had previously held the reins in the house took them up again, but her determination to restore order in it was of no avail, since with the news that kept arriving, we were all in more of an uproar than ever.

Poor me, caught between the two warring factions! As though my appointed tasks of bringing in wood, sweeping, scrubbing, lending a helping hand wherever needed were not enough, I was now being asked to spy. I never wanted to do such a thing, nor did I want to take part in violent arguments that more often than not ended in blows.

Our guest was by no means the least fervid participant in all that. Paying out of her own purse, she hired herself a private courier who once a week brought her, from the city where it was being held, a detailed report of how the trial by the Holy Tribunal was going.

She no doubt thought that if our two sisters were condemned, in just a few months' time she would end up becoming the mistress and head of the community in view of the precarious state of health of the old prioress.

But the old prioress stood her ground, patiently put up with disputes and rivalries, or at least never complained to the others or to me as many a time I helped her make her way painfully up the staircases. From one day to the next that sea of wrath that set the sisters against each other extended its dominion, leading to heated words and even to dishonest intentions. The total disregard for the rule of the house, the hope of news that would favor one faction or the other, the selfish interests of each and all in favor of our guest or against her made the convent and its hours not so much a haven of prayer as a cruel battlefield.

That year not even the procession of the patron saint of the house was held. That was because the enemies of our saintly sister hid his garments and adornments in an attic, and despite the fact that their rivals eventually found them, the house was in such turmoil that the prioress resigned herself to celebrating only a simple mass, as though it were merely another ordinary day in the week.

Our chaplain's exhortations were unavailing. His most reasoned arguments were met with a chorus of coughs and hisses, with murmurs, grumbling, and derisive handclapping on the part of the most rebellious of the sisters. Seeing all of them thus confronting each other, insulting each other with such violent passion, a person began to wonder whether they were daughters of Our Lord or devotees of Satan himself. Better a slave, a simpleton, a humble lay sister than a vessel of wrath like those wretched creatures. To the primary reasons for that interminable war others of a very different nature came to be added, directed in the most crude fashion against our guest's father. The sisters from families who were tenants on his estates swore that their fathers would rather be vassals of the king than serve such a tyrannical master. It would be a sad thing if all those favors he had promised the house, all that luxury displayed by such an illustrious sister came from having subjected the poor to gibbets, pillories, and constables, contravening all justice, flouting all established rights.

They said that his tenants, forced to pay higher and higher taxes, continually rebelled, that this was the real reason for the perpetual strife on his holdings and estates, rather than the fact that they rose up in revolt against the king, who in any case exacted much less of them. This state of affairs had given rise to violent unrest and rancors on every hand, and the abandonment of inherited lands that our protector then gave over to more docile and weaker vassals. Hence his holdings grew after every campaign that he successfully waged. The former tenants did everything in their power to see that their protests reached the ears of the king, but since he was at court, he was too far away and the men-at-arms of our protector too close at hand and readily available.

They recounted such things even in his daughter's presence, but she turned a deaf ear, pretending that her thoughts were entirely elsewhere, just as in the matter of the wounds she was the secret moving force behind a passionate, tragic battle that destroyed all discipline in the house.

Here in this solitude amid which I find myself, the days follow one upon the other, so indistinguishable from the nights that only the arrival of newcomers tells me that life goes on. An iron grille at the entrance to the courtyard can be heard opening, and shortly thereafter the sound of footsteps approaching, passing before my cell, and then dying away farther along as they stop before one or another of the other cells. Then the door, as heavy and massive as mine, with no doubt the same sort of narrow little window at the top that lets in only a dim light from outside, can be heard slamming shut.

At such times I wonder in which of these cells my sister is, what walls have swallowed up her sighs, whether her fate is similar to mine. Since I can no longer see her image in my mind's eye, I would like to hear her voice, but such a hope seems useless to me, unless they put us on trial together or some kindly keeper is willing to bring me news of what her life is like. My efforts to find a tiny crack, some old peephole through which to spy on what is happening in the courtyard, have been fruitless. It is plain to see what extraordinary lengths the Tribunal goes to in order to keep the various prisoners separate, in the twofold loneliness of silence and darkness.

It is midwinter now. Everything sweats with the dampness; the ceiling drips, garments are wet through, and one's flesh is numb from the cold. Since the costs of my stay here must be paid for by the order, it is not surprising that I am brought very little food, that there is never any meat, and that a little basket of oil, salt pork, and vinegar arrives only very seldom. Neither the wretched bed-covering that they gave me the first days, nor the blanket, the small rug, my thread-bare chemise are of much help in warding off the cold at night. Even though there in the convent we did not live with all the comforts enjoyed by our guest, I nonetheless confess that I sorely miss the stew from our kitchen, our warm brazier, the fruit from the garden.

But above and beyond such privations, even more than the dark solitude, more than the icy drafts from the passageways, what breaks my spirit is the lack of news: not knowing what we are accused of, what they know about us, what power holds sway over us, whose denunciation brought us here.

There is not a sign of anyone, no one comes to present reasons either for or against anything, the only person I see is the keeper who brings me food and water and takes the toilet jar away with him once a week. They neither harass me nor summon me; even the saint's faithful followers will soon forget me. The hours drag on, like a cluster of grapes that can never be consumed, that keeps eternally growing and thriving, as on this black shore where my soul has halted, in this icy awareness of my flesh, each moment that slips and falls away is a dull desire to die, to have done with a dream that is not a dream.

But it is truly said that the Lord never ravages the heart of hearts of His humble creatures. After Christmas, my door finally opened, and I was brought the first of the admonitions. Very courteously, though in grave, solemn voices, I was urged by the familiars to tell the truth, to hide nothing nor keep anything to myself, to trust in the mercy of the Holy Tribunal, which was competent to hear me and prepared to judge me.

I said nothing in reply. Alone, with no one to consult, with no more light of understanding than that brought me by the sermons of the house and a few pious books, what reply could I have given them? What can I do other than to remain silent when I am not even told how I am in error? For which of my many sins am I being judged? Better to wait till the next occasion if my courage is up to it, if the second admonition arrives, if my sister has not already confessed to the truth, her truth, the falsehood of the two of us that may lead both of us to the stake.

Chapter Seven

SHE is sitting in silence with her bandaged arms peeking out from beneath her mantle like the white Saint Andrew's cross that they paint on the backs of those delivered over to the secular Tribunal to be condemned. She barely glances at the familiar who is reading aloud the charges against her, very slowly, lingering over each detail. According to these charges, the accused suffers from prolonged and profound ecstasies in which she completely loses her senses and her memory, and once she has come out of them, she firmly maintains that she has had dealings and been in conversation with Jesus Christ Our Lord.

"Do you admit having so affirmed?"

"I never said such a thing," the accused replies in a soft, gentle voice that can barely be heard.

"Raise your voice. This Tribunal must record your statement."

"I said," she repeats, raising her voice with an effort, "that no such words ever came from my mouth."

"You did not see Our Lord?"

"I never saw Him. That too is not true."

"Not even in your dreams?"

This time she denies the charge with a forceful gesture, burying her head in her hands.

"What importance can it have if she saw Him in her dreams?" her defender interjects. "We would be better advised to confine ourselves to what the witnesses affirm, to what the accused did or saw while in full possession of her faculties."

But the prosecutor doesn't give an inch. He searches among the papers on his table, examines some of them, and stubbornly continues the interrogation:

"There are also witnesses who declare that they have seen various radiant lights emanating from her body. What does the accused have to say?"

"How would I be able to see them, if they were emanating from my body?"

"But do you admit that others might have been able to see them?"

"That may well be. I have no idea of what other eyes see— only my own."

"They also state that you cured a sick child."

"I make no such assertion. Many people come to the grille at the convent. It is not easy to determine through the grille whether they are sick or healthy."

"Does the accused touch them with her hands?"

"To my knowledge, caressing a child is not against dogma. Our Lord always sought to have them near Him."

"But did you succeed in curing any of them?"

The accused again does not answer, turning her eyes away from the shabby velvet cloth covering the prosecutor's table. She is heard to sigh as the latter insistently presses his point:

216

"The witnesses so state."

"You may believe them if you wish."

The prosecutor has taken her words as a challenge. He has turned toward the Tribunal, where the notary carefully takes down all testimony, word for word, and in an even, deliberate voice, as is appropriate since he is addressing his superiors, the prosecutor announces that he will read aloud from the register of depositions in which the pertinent facts are recorded.

"I"—he does not reveal the name—"an inhabitant of this town, declare and swear before this Tribunal to the following facts: that having come with my son, aged ten, who was suffering from a quartan ague, to the aforesaid convent, I had him touch the saint's hands through the grille, wherefore and thenceforth, as everyone could see, he was rid of his fevers, and at present is as strong and healthy as was our fervent wish."

The prosecutor raised his eyes to see the effect of these words on the Tribunal.

"Twenty other witnesses signed this declaration along with the parents. We also have other depositions at hand that recount all sorts of special gifts," he adds.

The judge contemplates the ray of light that serves to tell what time it is in the chamber, a beam in the form of a cross that shines down onto the stone labs of the floor through the tiny window behind him. He apparently decides that the sun is reaching its zenith, and struggling mightily to shake off his vague drowsiness, he begins to ask questions, still half-asleep.

"What sort of gifts are recounted in these declarations?"

"An entire session would be required to enumerate all of them."

The judge appears to be lost in thought once more, and addressing the accused again, he asks:

"So then, you possess the gift of working miracles?"

"How would I know?"

"Are you capable of healing illnesses, saving harvests, causing demons to depart from people's bodies?"

"Your Excellency, my answer is the same one as that to the previous questions. I know nothing of these gifts that I am said to possess. I have no knowledge of them, much less of this talk of harvests and demons."

"But you grant that such a thing is possible."

"Illustrious judges," the defender again interjects in a most circumspect manner, "I pray you to pardon my words and forgive me if in any way they are lacking in the respect due such an august Tribunal. What is here being judged and debated are not the prodigies that may or may not have occurred in that house, but whether or not they were really due to the gift that has been attributed to the accused. As she has assured you, she in no way accepts these prodigies as her doing."

"Nor does she reject that possibility."

"The testimony cannot be regarded as certain fact however."

"The witnesses are from families who have been Christians for generations."

"Even so. They too may fall into error through an excess of zeal. Sometimes a conversation, a single word wrongly interpreted may give rise to an unjust condemnation. No one, not even the most humble of the sons of God should find himself deprived of the benefit of doubt. It is my considered opinion that other new witnesses, whom I myself am willing to produce, should be heard."

The Tribunal agreed that he might present them, and hence the trial was carried over. The saint's fame thereupon spread beyond the city, eventually reaching the lands bordering on the capital. The king's highway now became an unending jubilee, full each day of carts, coaches, people on foot, clerics, and high-born gentlemen seeking to recover their health or merely in search of diversion, eager to possess the image of the accused and her miracles, which her many devotees sold in great quantities, in both painted and carved form. Soon there was not a single woman's skirt, man's garment, or cleric's habit that did not have pinned to it a cross or medal or bit of ribbon with the saint's hastily painted portrait on it, showing beams of light shining forth from her hands.

I, on the other hand, go completely unnoticed; it would appear that not even the Tribunal remembers my existence. Already winter is stealing away in the naked silence of the courtyards. The hoarfrost melts and drips monotonously each morning, and the snow merely threatens to fall from a sky so low that I can almost feel its weight there beyond my window.

We are about to receive our third admonition, yet the prosecutor still has not summoned me before him. Not one word has been said to me about the matter of the wounds, the only thing for which in all conscience and as best my memory serves me, I might possibly be denounced and condemned. I have not been told whether I will have someone to defend me before the Tribunal, or when the trial will be, or who will decide my fate. They have surrounded me with a wall of silence that I try to break through by forgetting the things of this world, the happy days, the slights of the past, just as my sister once enjoined me to do, struggling against the wish to die, fighting off my fears. But as the days pass and disappear from memory, my body and my reason falter, above all since our house stopped paying for my maintenance. We are now dependent upon the charity of the Holy Tribunal; we earn the straw on which we sleep and the soup that is brought to us by the work that we do.

Such tasks, however, neither repel me nor humiliate me; rather, they satisfy my desire to suffer, born anew within me as each day dawns. It is such a cruel torturer that the most thankless work is welcome. Mending, sweeping, brushing away cobwebs, scrubbing the chamber pot is all agreeable medicine for this new state in which I feel once again, along with the terrible loneliness, the sweet prick of the thorn of melancholy. My body is so weak and exhausted that I fear I shall collapse on this miserable straw pallet and never rise from it again. A sad end that at times satisfies me nonetheless.

But if I die without our having won a victory, what will happen to the house? Where will our protector proceed to bestow his favor? As my anxieties mount, the more I think of my defeat, the longer the days become, within me and without, in the empty passageways, where only the distant ringing of a bell, whispered conversations, and the sound of footfalls tell me that other trials are taking place, other judgments being pondered and arrived at long before ours.

In the second locutory, reserved for the nobility, full of portraits, reliquaries, and crosses that completely cover every inch of the whitewashed walls, the guest of the house is awaiting her courier, glancing in passing at the portraits of former prioresses, the cracks in the ceiling, the eagles of the choir desk that once upon a time presided over the offices of the house. She paces slowly back and forth across the broken tiles, the crumbling mortar that once held them together, the tiny cocoons of caterpillars. She glances at the proud, serene faces, enveloped in black mantles, some of them half effaced, as though they had vanished. She barely reads their names. In the end they are all one; all that matters is their office and their accession to it, one after the other along the wall as in life. As the two weights of the clock pull time slowly along to the tick of the pendulum, her impatience grows, her eyes searching, peering into the darkness beyond the grille with its double row of bars bristling with nails. More than threats, they become a symbol. No one can remain pinned to the grille on them, they are too big and massive, and at the same time as easy to escape from as the very walls themselves, so ancient that they have caved in. Like the entire house, they are there to serve as a warning to the humble, a reminder rather than a safeguard since there is little stored up inside them save tedium in the afternoons and cold in the morning.

There are no visits from gallant suitors, no presents, no little notes with warm words between the lines, enticements to passion—merely poor relatives, wretched family members who on departing in the afternoon leave in the turning-box their offering of chickens and lambs.

With the saint far away now, the darkness on the other side of the grille seems continually deserted. It is as though the entire town had gone off after her, as though all her devout followers had agreed to meet outside the Tribunal, convinced that the saint's fate was their fate, that the salvation of the entire city depended on her salvation. It is of no use to admonish people, to preach sermons to them, to explain that prodigies such as this are born and die by the hundreds each day in any number of other convents and abbeys. It is useless, because nobody is familiar with anything but his own small plot of ground, and the world ends just a little way beyond his untilled fields or his pasture land.

Better to remain silent, to visit the refectory only rarely, to abandon the choir, partly out of disdain and partly out of boredom, to listen to the stories the others invent out of the whole cloth, to wait, as now, for the door outside to creak on its hinges, announcing that the courier is arriving as punctually as usual.

Suddenly the wooden steps of the stairway resound with footfalls and the door opens. Someone immediately closes it again from outside. The courier, scarcely more than a youngster, with his boots still covered with mud and his eyes reddened from the wind, is standing there inside. Once a door opens somewhere and lets in a little light, he strides toward the grille as though following a path with which he is familiar. On the other side the curtain stirs and immediately the two of them, courier and mistress, are face to face, like a lover and his lady, on either side of the grille.

The lad has scarcely caught his breath when his mistress's voice begins to ply him with questions in the darkness.

"How is the trial going? Are the admonitions over and done with?"

"The final one was more than a week ago. At least as far as the saint is concerned."

"Has the accusation been read?"

"It has. Witnesses are now being heard. The verdict will depend in large part on their declarations. The Tribunal has appointed a defender for her, although according to what people say, he's of little help in such cases."

"Well then, what does help?"

"Other new witnesses to contradict the previous ones, milady. But hunting them up takes work and presupposes that they'll be well paid. It's not going to be an easy way to convince the Tribunal."

"Have depositions been taken from the accused?"

"Apparently they've taken the saint's. And in view of her position of importance in the church hierarchy, they've granted her the special favor of informing her of the charges against her, though as is well-known, they are not ordinarily that considerate. But this news, like all the rest that I've brought you, is not at all certain."

"You've brought me very little, when I'd hoped for so much more."

"If it were in my power, milady, I would bring you

the trial records themselves, but you know what great danger that involves. I wouldn't like to end up with my bones in their jails, where as the saying has it, you know when it is that you enter them but have no idea when you'll get out of them."

The courier, who was quite tired, was already on his way out when, retracing his steps, he raised his face, still covered with dust and badly sunburned from his journey.

"What I can definitely assure you, because I saw it with my own eyes, is that many people are talking about forming a brotherhood with her as their patroness."

"The authorities will keep her locked up rather than allow such nonsense."

"The one scarcely precludes the other, milady. It is far easier to say that than it is to defy the wrath of the faithful. I'm merely reporting what I have seen: that her portrait is well on its way to being displayed on altars. People are merely waiting for the Tribunal to pronounce judgment."

The guest of the house said nothing as she pondered the words of the lad, who was leaving as discreetly as he had come. She was so upset that she did not hear the sound of the prioress's footsteps approaching, the light touch of the old woman's hand on her shoulder, or her voice asking:

"Has news of the trial arrived?"

The guest had not yet answered as the two of them began walking through the cloister together, surrounded by the other sisters, as they headed for the guest's cell where her maidservant was setting the table.

"What news is there? Are they going to let the saint go free?"

"Have the final deliberations begun?"

"Was the verdict for or against her?"

"Is it true that they've adjourned her case indefinitely?"

The prioress tried in vain to disperse her flock.

"Sisters, be on your way. It's time you were heading downstairs to the refectory."

But her efforts were of no avail. The silence of the older sisters was as eloquent as the shouts and murmurs of the younger ones.

"Let her tell us if there's any news."

"Let us know at least if they've decided to punish her or to honor her."

"You'll know soon."

"Tonight, Mother?"

"Tonight or tomorrow. I promise you that we won't keep any news that we receive to ourselves."

The flock ceased their entreaties, albeit unwillingly, until finally, trusting in their faith in the old prioress and the better judgment of the older sisters, they retraced their steps and headed toward the refectory, though not without casting frequent backward glances at the prioress as she entered the distinguished guest's cell.

Once inside, the two of them fell silent, the one meditating, the other opposite her lost in anxious thought. The guest offered the prioress a little basket of fruit which the old woman refused, barely glancing at it, her attention fixed solely on the words that would be forthcoming. Her eyes traveled from the lady to the maidservant, from the table to the dishes that little by little were set out till they covered the entire tablecloth.

"The fame of our sister is spreading by the day," the guest of the house said at last, breaking the silence. "If the Tribunal does not condemn her, I am very much afraid that we have a saint on our hands whose reputation has increased and multiplied, a hundred times more famous than when she left this house."

"I do not think that they will absolve her," the old woman answered.

"They can also suspend their sentence indefinitely so as to prevent her from appealing their verdict."

"And what does that matter to the Tribunal? She can appeal if she so chooses. In any event the final verdict will be a long time in coming; her appeal will be sent to the Supreme Tribunal, where it will drag on for two or three years."

"And what will we do meanwhile? If she gets off free, her cause will have prevailed and her fame grown even greater. Only a forthright condemnation will favor our interests."

The old prioress appeared to be lost in thought. Her eyes were now focused beyond the velvets and damasks, gazing at the timid sun breaking through the clouds, faintheartedly presaging spring.

"When do you think the formal reconciliation will take place?"

The guest's gaze sought the other woman's, clouded and filled with sadness.

"Who can say? In view of her status and office, they

cannot confiscate her possessions or sentence her to wear a sanbenito, or send her to the galleys, or flog her. The most they can do is to sentence her to incarceration for life."

"And does that seem to you a mild punishment?"

"I would judge it a harsh one if it proved to be one she really served, but all of us know that the Tribunal is short of prisons. There are so many accused that their cells are full. Their life sentences seldom go beyond two or three years' imprisonment. Hence we ought not to be surprised if in the end they return her to us, reconciled and repentant, but as saintly as before in the eyes of all of those who have faith in her."

She paused, and then added, in a graver tone of voice:

"All of this holds true only if they decide not to put her to death. Repenting or not, saving her life or being burned at the stake depends on her."

The maidservant came and went, well trained to serve unobtrusively, without making her presence noted in the pauses in the conversation, her fingers barely touching the silver service, with neither undue haste or delay.

"I trust Your Mercy will not repent."

The prioress swiftly raised her eyes.

"What reason would I have for so doing? My conscience is as clear and as unburdened by guilt as on the first day. I testified only to the truth, to what happened in this house once those wounds made their appearance."

"What you say is most praiseworthy," the other answered readily. "But as Your Mercy knows, the truth has not just one face but many. It is as protean as the intentions of the one who decides to use it for his or her own ends."

"Was what I heard from the accused's own lips, when she was lost in dreams, not true then?"

"Were those the dreams you testified to in your letter?"

The prioress nodded reluctantly this time, as the guest sitting opposite her listened with a satisfied air.

"Well then," she murmured, "we can only believe that they will find her guilty." Her tone of voice suddenly became more affable. "Why are you of such troubled mind? Thanks to your testimony, along with that of many others that will surely be forthcoming, you have rendered a great service to this convent and to the order."

"And Your Mercy will eventually be prioress," the old woman said in conclusion.

"And what fault is there in that? My father taught me that there are only two overriding reasons that make this world go round. The first is the desire for power and the second the thirst for glory—and in most instances, they are one and the same."

"But what sort of glory do you think you will find here, coming as you did from the court? What sort of fame can await you in this miserable house?"

The guest's eyes took in, in a single glance, her beautifully appointed cell, her soft bed, the heavy draperies, the viands on the table. And as it embraced the submissive maidservant and the silent prioress as well, she murmured to herself:

"As Our Lord said: my kingdom is not of this world. It is not to be found here in this empty, foolish house. Wait until the undertaking that we have embarked upon together is brought to a conclusion, and I will reveal my reasons to you. Meanwhile, you may be certain that if you serve me as you have thus far, I shall not forget you when that hour comes."

The familiars of the Tribunal, solemn, ceremonious, grave, take their places on the platform. The time that this trial has dragged on weighs heavily on them as well. Their gaze sweeps past the defense, the prosecutor, and the accused, searching beyond them in the dark shadows at the far end of the hall for some unexpected turn of events before the usual prayer begins their labors, which are barely halfway over, having been delayed by interminable testimony, preliminary hearings, and the readings of charges. So many accused have already filed before their eyes, in this same dimly lighted audience chamber, that they mingle and blend into one: new Christians, lustful clerics, convicted Lutherans delivered over to the secular arm, all of them united together in a common purgatory, the path to life or to hell.

Once the prayer has ended and those present have fallen silent once again, the chief judge asks that the last remaining charges that have not yet been heard be read aloud.

"The last one is the most important. It has to do with the stigmata, those wounds that are said to appear in her hands every so often. According to the sworn testimony of one witness, the accused was heard to say that she receives them from Our Lord."

"Is that true?" the judge asks the accused.

"I never said such a thing."

"Nonetheless, I have such testimony here before me, just as I have read it."

The prosecutor holds up before the Tribunal the book whose double pages are full of minute, crabbed notations. The familiars' eyes, the judge's, turn dully from the pages to the accused's barely visible arms, hidden by the folds of her habit.

"Let the acused bear in mind that if she acknowledges her error, she may save her life."

"Illustrious members of the Tribunal," her defender interjects, in the same respectful tone as usual, "the accused is cognizant of the benefits she may gain thereby."

"Very well then," the prosecutor continues. "This being the case, I will put the matter another way. The accused denies having affirmed that the aforementioned wounds were the work of Our Lord."

"That is so."

"But when the community recognized them as such, neither did she raise any objection."

The saint remains silent. From far in the distance there comes the sound of a bell, marking off the time as everyone awaits her answer, long moments that cause the solemn expressions of the judges on the bench to become more animated.

"The Tribunal is awaiting your answer."

"I have said nothing, it is true."

The prosecutor sets the book down on the table, and with a whirl of his mantle states, without turning round:

"Wherefrom it may be deduced that she lied by omission."

"Illustrous members of the Tribunal," the defender replies, "since the matter at hand is of such a special nature, it is necessary to presume that the accused kept silent merely out of a lack of knowledge."

There is no answer from the judges' bench. At times the faces on the platform consult each other in a low voice, disagree, agree, or remain mute in the face of the arguments that the prosecutor sets forth one by one, filling the chamber with his calm, intermittent voice.

"In view of the rank held by the accused in the church hierarchy," he goes on, "I for my part am willing to grant that she remained silent out of circumspection, albeit this circumspection, naturally, did not prevent her from accepting the office of prioress which no doubt those wounds earned her."

"What reason would I have had to decline the office?"

"The Tribunal grants your point. Let us go on to the other declarations."

The prosecutor picks up the book again. He holds it up before those present and says:

"I have here the most important testimony. That of a person very close to the accused."

The saint totters on her feet. It is necessary for the bailiff to bring her a backless chair to sit on, as those present appear for the first time to turn their attention to her adversary, who is struggling with the many pages of the trial record as he explains:

"This is a witness who has lived in extremely close association with the accused, a person whose position places her beyond all suspicion. Her testimony reads: 'Since our convent was in such a precarious state, it is common knowledge that the sister began to ponder whether it would not be helpful to feign some extraordinary event which, as usually happens in such cases, would bring us more substantial aid from our benefactors. It is said, and there are those willing to swear, that with the help of her accomplice she herself made those wounds in her hands, which she thereafter caused to bleed as much and as often as was necessary for her purposes.' "

Page after page, pause after pause, the prosecutor's voice captures the entire attention of everyone in the room as he reads this testimony. Even the saint listens intently.

Outside, the bell stops ringing, and the sound of the birds in the cloister can scarcely be heard in the chamber. The testimony little by little creates around the accused a wall even thicker than the massive walls of the prison. She appears to be indifferent to her fate now, alone and resigned as the words follow endlessly one upon the other, not so much read as recited in a dull monotone. The familiars barely look at each other, whisper or comment to each other now; the voice is at once a prosecutor and a defender as it describes the facts in minute detail.

"Hence, after a time, noting that her health was completely undermined, she sought relief from our surgeon who, placing his knowledge at her service and in secret, tried a drastic remedy to arrest her illness, that had left her so prostrated that she had lost the use of her speech and her senses, becoming the victim of hallucinations. During them, in her sleep, she confessed on various occasions everything herewith declared, for the good of the community and for the greater enlightenment of this Holy Tribunal within whose competence the hearing and weighing of such facts falls."

"Has the surgeon been sent for?" the judge asks, and as the bailiff nods, he orders the accused:

"Approach the Tribunal. Let us see those hands."

Very slowly the bandages begin one by one to fall away. From their folds stained with dark red blood, filthy with dust and dried clots, the flesh, dead now, comes to light and life for the last time, from the palm of her hand to her elbow, abused, mortified, turned into hard roots of skin only partially concealed by gnarled tendons resembling vine shoots. Again the Tribunal comes to life. This time it is partly hostile fear, partly mistrust of their own venal feelings of compassion that makes their eyes gleam watchfully.

"You may conceal them from sight again."

And as the hands disappear once more, the doctor approaches, following the bailiff. He too is fearful, remains silent, glances all around when he is asked why he tried to close the wounds.

"I thought that if they were caused by supernatural forces, I would lose nothing if I failed. If, on the other hand, they were due to other, lesser causes, I might be able to restore the patient's health, thereby fulfilling my duty as a physician and being of service to the community."

"What do you mean precisely by lesser causes?"

"An accident, or merely some sort of illness."

"In your opinion, can that be the origin of them?"

"My knowledge does not extend beyond the physical health of the body."

"Illustrious members of the Tribunal," the prosecutor interrupts, "may I ask this man a question?"

More hesitation, and then once the Tribunal grants its permission, he turns to the surgeon and asks:

"Have you seen the hands of the accused today?"

"The last time I saw them was nearly a year ago, when I proceeded to cauterize them."

"Do you wish to examine them again now?"

"I am willing to do so if the Tribunal deems it necessary."

"Let us suppose that the accused were in danger of dying. According to the one criterion on which you base your practice, namely the physical health of the patient alone, what would you do? Arrest the illness or allow it to threaten her life?"

"I am not able to answer. The two alternatives you propose are extreme cases."

"I assure you that they are not."

The surgeon hesitates. His eyes seek the accused, whose face he can barely see in the darkness, and then turn away to look at the judges, who are attentively awaiting his reply.

"If her health, her life were in danger, my duty would be to try to cure her."

"And if the wounds were supernatural? I remind you that your previous treatment of them did little good."

"I would try nonetheless. As you are well aware, I am bound by my oath as a physician."

"Then it makes no difference. That is to say, according to the science of which you are a practitioner, you consider such wounds in any event to be natural, ones owed to what you call lesser causes."

The prosecutor now approaches the judges' bench, and with his gaze fixed on the mountain of documents that have accumulated in the course of the trial, he murmurs in a solemn tone of voice, turning toward those present in the chamber:

"I ask the illustrious notary of this high Tribunal to take due and proper note of the fact that the surgeon himself is today of the opinion that these signs are natural—albeit in a poisoned state at present—and would appear to be wounds inflicted upon herself by the accused, as is borne out by the testimony appended to the record of these proceedings. We therefore recommend that the case be transferred to the Council of Qualifications, in order that this latter may be good enough to indicate whether it finds signs or notable suspicion of an offense against faith, heresy, blasphemy, or error, and should it find that there be such, hand down the pertinent sentence."

Time, like winter, fled, without any important news. The snow retreated to high ground. There were few blinding flashes of lightning now, only faint discharges in the late afternoon. The city now lay open to the slow processions of wagons heading for markets inland, to the dense herds of sheep trembling on patches of lingering hoarfrost, to the loud pealing of bells.

The fields came alive once more with great droves of sheep and cattle and noisy gangs of boys who came down from the city to do battle, their contests usually ending in clumsy exchanges of blows and stupid threats. One boy with his face slashed was brought to the convent so that the saint would heal the wound. A poor choice of a remedy, seeing as how she was with her companion in prison, heaven only knew for how long! They'd come looking for the wrong surgeon when not even our guest had any news as to whether she was about to go to the stake, whether she and her companion were being turned over to the secular arm.

In time the news made the rounds that neither of the two would be coming back. That news had not come by way of the courier's valise, nor a visit from an official of the Tribunal, nor even of one of the many transporters of goods, always up to date on the latest news from the court, who happened to pass by. And yet everyone who lived inside the walls, clerics and peasants, woke up one morning convinced that they would never see the saint again, that she was going to be condemned to perpetual exile.

The sisters were even more surprised when, on hearing a loud clamor coming from the other side of the latticed windows, they peeked out and saw that new multitude exactly like the processions of bygone days, a crowd of townspeople slowly approaching, amid laments and prayers, to ask for one last favor, a little white lie capable of consoling their hearts. But the fate of the saint did not lie there; it no longer depended on the house now. Her return or her disappearance forever was still in the hands of that distant Tribunal whose verdict would be known some day.

Once it had passed judgment, the convent would learn of its decision without the need for any sort of revelation save the seal and the signature of the judges.

True or not, the news poked up the embers in the house, the heated feelings, not yet dead, with regard to the prioress, the hostility against the guest, whom many accused of harboring ill-will against the saint, of being vain and ambitious. Soon voices were raised asking who it was who had been the source of the testimony against the new prioress, who was benefiting most from her long absence. And since such suspicions invariably centered on the same person, or rather, on the same two persons, that rumor born of wrath and hope gradually drove the old prioress to take refuge in her cell. Though she seldom showed her face, she did appear at times to speak with those sisters who loudly demanded news of the fate of the two accused sisters.

The hostility reached such a point that there were sisters who turned their back on her in private, and no one would sit next to her in the refectory, thereby disregarding the rules of the house. Very shortly, what with one silence after another, one protest after another, her courage failed her, her health declined, and her spirits flagged, until finally she remained in bed for days on end. She could now feel the hatred of the others spying on her at night from outside, through the cracks in the door.

"Who's that? Who's there?" she would mutter, her eyes searching the darkness.

And it was only the March wind that sent back, as always, its angry reply.

Grateful for the favor she had shown me by taking me back in when I returned to the convent like the prodigal son, when I was not on duty at the main door I was the only one who bothered to bring her meals to her. None of the other sisters chided me for so doing, but I sensed that they were not pleased to see me take the badly prepared food in to her, seasoned with a bit of conversation and company.

Only rarely were there signs of life at her door, in the form of the visit of the chaplain, who was in the habit of hearing her confession, but that sacrament now began to pile up torment upon torment, doubt upon doubt, within her soul. He listened in silence to the weary murmur of her lips: always the same faults, an old and all too familiar story now, as worn out as she herself was. Every so often he would nod his head and on giving her his absolution set her some minor penance, after the ritual question:

"Have you nothing else to tell me?"

And the old prioress answered no, time after time.

The chaplain's patience, his friendship with her that went back so many years, were unavailing. Her sin, the fault he kept expecting her to confess never came forth from her lips, however much he pressed her, as though her last remaining strength were causing her to rebel, to stand her ground, ever since the day the community had abandoned her.

"Is there no grave fault that you accuse yourself of?"

And the mute reply of her lips was accompanied by an adamant gesture to indicate that her confession had ended. Then when the chaplain had left, there began once more that concert of whispers and footsteps, of eyes spying from outside on her state of health, her sleeplessness, the food she had been unable to get down, the bucket with the few drops of water in it drying up, the motionless beads of her rosary, the sleeves of her cilice lying atop the pale expanse of sheets as lifeless as an untilled field.

She lay there day after day, not moving, clinging to her throne of planks and bedcovers, swathed in her pride, with only her eyes alive, burning with fever by midafternoon. The entire house gravitated around her, the fate of the saint, the rancor of the latter's faithful, her terrifying abandonment, and the dream of the daughter of our long-standing protector which was about to be realized, for upon the death of the old prioress she would undoubtedly see her hopes fulfilled. For her too, for no apparent reason since the courier kept returning with nothing to report, the fate of the two sisters seemed to be forgotten, a foregone conclusion.

Many times, walking through the cloister on my way to the garden with my basket of laundry on my head, I caught a glimpse of her in her cell, closeted with her servant and friend. Dressed in her most elegant attire, sitting in front of the mirror that sent her back the reflection of her young, strong face, her delicate mouth, and her alert eyes, she seemed to be awaiting the moment when the bell or her courier or the voice of her faithful followers would come to announce to her that her reign was beginning, that her will to rule supreme and her ambition had reached full flower and were about to bear abundant fruit.

Lord in heaven, into what cruel exile you have cast me, with what miseries you chastise me in this forbidding loneliness to which I am condemned! The days follow one upon the other beyond the walls of my cell, in patios and passageways, in the city full of pleasure-gardens and tree-lined promenades that I crossed one day. Here however almost no light enters save through the narrow little window, beyond which heavy footsteps come and go, though I have no way of knowing whether they are heading toward the scaffold or toward hope.

From time to time a door opens, voices resound in the corridor and a dull clanking of irons and chains mingles with the cooing of doves and the hoarse broken cries of crows.

Lord in heaven, I turn unto Thee these useless eyes that have almost nothing to feed upon, only darkness and emptiness and the dim outlines of dripping walls. They are almost worthless to me, as wavering as my footsteps on the stone floor, as dull as the sense of touch of my rough hands. In this solitude only my sense of hearing grows sharper, more acute, already distinguishing very clearly the arrival of spring by the sound of the wind or the birds, of summer in the deafening chirr of the cicadas, of autumn that dwells eternally in the steely voice of the pines. It is as though with time my hearing is being transformed, becoming a spy or a prophet, engraving on my memory the arrogant footfalls of the bailiff, the peremptory hands of the guards, the fearful shuffle of the prisoners, their joyful trot if they are heading for freedom, their subdued solemnity if they are heading for the Holy Tribunal.

And what will my footsteps sound like? In what manner will I pass through this door? What will be my demeanor as I accompany my guards? Will I leave this prison dead or alive, humiliated or yoked forever to the dignity and destiny of my sister? Like the seasons, like the time for sowing, growing, reaping, one day treads upon the heels of another, all of them indifferent to our destiny. What fate awaits us? What fate awaits those others whose footsteps or coughs or belches I hear outside my door at daybreak? How will it end, this time that makes us brothers and sisters to each other in spirit and unites us? Each time that my keeper appears, after announcing himself by loudly shooting the bolts of my cell, I ask him about his other charges. But he says nothing, assures me that he knows nothing, that there are so many who are transferred to another prison or freed, so many taken away to be sentenced or put to death, that he can scarcely keep track of them. Nor does he have any news of my sister; he has no idea if she is still here or if the Tribunal has ordered her transferred somewhere else. But since the two of us were summoned before it at the same time, we are no doubt to be condemned or let go together as well.

True or not, something within me tells me that I am sharing this waiting, this time of imprisonment with her, that it is hers as well, that it belongs to both of us like that other time, those happy years in the garden and the convent cell. The demon who denounced us may ensure our defeat but cannot separate us, for love thrives amid misfortune, grows amid terrible vicissitudes, and if in the end we are forced to deliver our souls into the hands of the Almighty, He who understands and knows everything, the two of us will die together despite those who denounced us.

The hardest thing to bear is not the scarcity of bread, of salt, the black cold of this cell in winter, or not being able to hear mass or receive the sacraments. May the Lord forgive me, but of all my many trials what is most difficult to bear is this darkness that is growing with time, these useless eyes whose failing powers have gradually been taken over by my sense of touch and hearing. What must those other prisons be like, the royal dungeons, when there are prisoners who confess to heresy so as to be sent to these! How little we know of the world, of the lot of so many who are eager to pass on to the other world so as to be relieved of their suffering by death!

One of those who was lacking in faith, bereft of all hope, hanged himself. They had bound him to the rack, and at the very first turns, he began to ask what he had to confess in order to have his bonds loosened. But our Tribunal does not wish to obtain confessions in this way. It wants the accused to set forth, of his own free will, everything that really happened. That is what they asked him to do, giving the rollers another turn. And the guard says that instead of admitting his errors, the man did nothing but ask for mercy, pleading that they free him from those cords that were biting deeper and deeper into his arms and legs. He cried out to the Lord, begged for His infinite mercy. Fighting to remain free, at times he declared that he acknowledged the truth of everything the witnesses had testified to, only to affirm his innocence again just a few moments later as the pain lessened. Then the torturer went on with his work, until his strength failed him, taking care not to endanger the life of the accused, or to damage any of his limbs permanently.

The secretary waited in vain alongside the rack, with his pen at the ready and sheets of blank paper before him. That mouth never uttered another word, not even to beg for mercy, as though the pain had suddenly sealed his throat. They took him back to his cell, and at midday when his keeper came to leave him his food he saw him swaying back and forth in the darkness. He was hanging from an esparto rope that he himself must have woven some time before without anyone's noticing.

What can his offense have been? Who could his accusers have been? Had he found himself here, like all the rest of us, because of a denunciation by witnesses whose names he never learned, whom he perhaps never saw, but whose testimony can prevail against the accused? A sad fate ours, marked by loneliness, if not by the greed and the fear of those who remain outside.

The guard, who has grown old in this corridor, giving rise to, or putting an end to such fearful dreams, recalls how many of those who have preceded us here arrived after being denounced by members of their own family or by neighbors, in search of vengeance or material gain. That was what happened to my father's village upon the arrival of the Holy Office. Who could possibly have told me that on the path of life I would be obliged to confront the risk of losing it!

Like a summer storm, there fell over our fields that dark cloud that goes by the name of the Edict of Faith, ordering that anyone who knew of a heretic or a Jew among his neighbors or in his own household was to denounce him; if he did not do so, he himself would be tried in turn. Though in the small villages in the country, the edict did not bring an abundant harvest, in the larger cities it caused many people to denounce others: sons accused their fathers, the poor the rich, and certain people even accused themselves, just a step ahead of those who were already dreaming of getting their hands on their possessions. Many homes were boarded up then, many estates confiscated, some forever, with the owner in prison, rich in material possessions and at the same time kept alive only by others' charity, or driven into exile and fallen into disgrace though his only sin was to have hoarded a few ducats in his house.

And the guard added that the worst of it was not that state of poverty to which so many were reduced, obliged to live on alms if the trial dragged on, but the obligation to denounce others, whether they were accomplices or not, in order to get themselves a less harsh sentence.

One day, when I praised him for his keen knowledge and judgment concerning a subject as weighty as that of our Tribunal, he finally confessed to me that he too had lived through such a critical moment. Denounced and eventually absolved, his case had dragged on for so long before being settled that when he returned to the world he found his house and lands sold, his wife gone off, and his sons scattered like a flock of sheep that has lost its shepherd. For some time he went about begging, coming to know what it was like to sleep on threshing floors of a summer night, and to be rudely awakened in a haystack of a winter morning. Until he came here.

"Why here, brother?" I asked him one day.

"What difference is there between this place and anywhere else? At my age they're all the same. The one thing I have left to hope for is that the Lord will call me to Him. The world here inside and the one outside are so much alike that it seems as though our Tribunal is exhausting its prosecutors and notaries for nothing. All of us, saints and heretics alike, will end up the same way, in the arms of death. And when all is said and done that's not the worst state."

"What's the worst then? Eternal hellfire?"

"Eternal hellfire is no more cruel than being burned to death at the stake. The worst thing about this world is being called into it, coming into it with the hope of being happy. We are brought here and then abandoned here, and it's here that we dance to heaven's tune till Judgment Day."

As I can barely see his face, I trust his voice, and find that what he says makes sense. He is one of the few who do not tremble with fear or plead or weep here; he is like an expanse of water on a summer day, at once perfectly calm and monotonous. Like the echoes in the corridor, like my fate, lingering on, enduring, entirely apart from me, distant, immutable.

As the columns of the cloister explain in stone, like the stubborn circling of the goshawks the months come and go, forming the turning wheel of the year, following the rhythm of the rain, the rise and fall of the rivers.

First comes January, the month closest to the door that leads to the passageway lined with cells; it has a double face, the first looking toward the year that is ending and the other toward the one that is beginning.

After it comes February, warming its feet next to the embers in its warm brazier, as we sisters are in the habit of doing between one prayer and another. It is followed by March, that prunes the vines when the broom in flower little by little tinges the woodlands with yellow.

It was under its protection, before April turns the hills into solid masses of color, that the old prioress delivered her soul to Our Lord God, one mild night with the moon turning the hillsides silver. As we returned from complin, we discovered her lying in her bed with her hands crossed on her breast, as though she were quite ready to be buried, far removed at last from conflicts and rancors. Her wide-open eyes with their fixed stare told us nothing as to what her end was like, whether she left this world comforted or full of remorse, bound for the kingdom where we are saved or on the road to the realm where we are damned. Nothing could be read in them, they seemed blank, emptier than her hands, so full of life still, resting motionless on the cross of her habit. Hence no one ever found out for certain whether it was her testimony that condemned the saint, or whether or not she came to repent her deed before sleep and death conspired to take her far from us.

The only one who might have known was the guest of the house, but she remained silent, detached if not indifferent, even as they laid her friend in the earth. Later however, in the chapter room, as arrangements for the forthcoming election for the vacant office were being discussed, her bustling about in search of news and votes, her promising of favors, her face, suddenly transformed, serene and smiling once again, were a sight to behold, the sisters said.

Like the breeze outside, she swept away bad memories with promises that silenced hostile murmurs; like melting snow suddenly become a free-flowing spring, she proclaimed that better times would come if she were chosen to head the house.

Little by little the small group of her firm supporters grew, becoming once again so numerous and closely knit that her victory appeared to be a foregone conclusion, but a few days before the vote was to be taken, someone started the rumor that the saint was returning.

Whether true or not, the news seemed to raise the saint's banner on high once more. It would be necessary to wait until the Tribunal had passed judgment upon her before taking away from her the office that the old prioress had occupied only on a temporary basis after the saint's imprisonment. Each time that the guest tried to speak up in the chapter, endeavoring to garner votes, a storm of coughs and hisses drowned out her voice until she was forced to fall silent, beet-red with rage and indignation. Despite her promises, which had soon been followed by outright threats, she was not able to make anyone heed her words save those sisters already won over to her cause. Nothing frightened off the others, above all the oldest sisters, who seemed to have made common cause with the accused. Although the house was falling apart by the day, with the garden still untended and the church a mere heap of ruins, it was necessary to wait, to appoint at the very most a council of elder sisters, of those with the greatest experience, who would keep the community going until the Tribunal pronounced judgment.

It was soon evident that the sisters were not acting as they were out of a love of truth, but out of hatred for someone whose attitude and possessions had made them aware of the misery of their lives, the falseness of their vocations, the wretchedness of their haven from the world. Perhaps if she had not come to the house, they would have died, not happy perhaps, but at least resigned to their lot, but that cell that in other days she had taken such great pleasure in showing off, her obedient maidservant, her elegant costumes, the sumptuous viands, the aromatic beverages, the crested and embroidered fillet round her hair, her polished mirrors and abundant larder loomed large in the eyes of those of us who had never known anything but rough serge and esparto grass, cilices, scourges, the bitter cold of the choir, or mortified flesh beneath our habits.

It was asking a great deal to expect us to swallow, on top of all that, her ordering us about, establishing our hours, amending our daily round of activities, correcting our every step. Such was the opinion we had all more or less arrived at as the day of the election drew near.

May came, a gallant cavalier in the cloister, with its half-overcast skies and its meadows dotted with flowers in full bloom. When June arrived, the first hot winds began to blow, and July brought in the harvest of wheat with sickles of lightning that from dawn on lighted up the heavy, lowering sky. The king's highway was deserted as it disappeared in the distance, weary, weighed down like a bad dream by a silence broken only by the creaking of heavily laden carts slowly lumbering along, full of golden sheaves, heading for bright sun-drenched threshing floors. The suffocating heat of mid-afternoon made the hills and springs in the valleys shimmer, and the convent fell asleep and dreamed, waiting for its fate to be determined, for a time or forever, who could say?

Tasks were done and prayers said without further question or command, at the sound of the bell ringing. My hands turned into prioresses, into the only voice respected and obeyed, save by our guest who had again

248

shut herself up in her chamber, showing her face only on rare occasions as she opened her door a crack to dispatch or receive, as always, her secret messages via her personal couriers.

But her letters, as we learned later, were no longer being sent off to the city where the saint was awaiting her sentence; our guest's chief concern lay elsewhere now. We in the community very soon learned the new destination that her messengers were bound for.

Very early one morning, as the sun broke through its cortege of clouds, another cortege appeared amid the dust and the vineyards, approaching at the slow pace of noble horsemen. That troop surely was not coming from either the court or the city where the Tribunal held its trials, but from still farther away. Small though it was, it seemed to loom larger and larger as it approached across the plain, an imposing troop riding in close formation.

Once it was close at hand, we soon guessed that it was our protector returning, and learned even sooner the reason for that unexpected return that had caused him to leave the still-burning embers of his campaign behind him. The moment I climbed down from the belfry and brought the sisters the news, some of them immediately grew more disheartened than ever, while others, few in number, felt new hope dawning. One or another of the sisters naturally took it upon herself to run tell his daughter who, as though she were expecting the news, had been lingering at the entrance to the patio when the troop drew up.

She stood there surrounded by the community, her demeanor so humbly obedient now that she appeared to be the new prioress already, the mistress of the house awaiting her father, who took her in his arms the moment he dismounted. The horsemen remained behind at the entrance, and the father, after finishing a light repast that we served him in the chapter room, in violation of the rules of the house, addressed us like a shepherd leading his flock:

"I have had news of the sad events that have taken place here since my last visit. May it please the Lord that they end happily, since my peace of mind and my devotion for this house depend in large measure on their outcome. As for the saint's trial, I am told that it is in expert hands. These learned men are quite capable of passing judgment as to whether or not a crime has been committed, and to what degree there has been a sin and a transgression against dogma in the community, who her accomplices were, and what punishment they deserve."

He spoke like a father who has been half deceived and half affronted. At times the flabby folds of his neck drooped down over his gorget as he shook with wrath. At times he seemed to lack air; his face grew red, and only a brief pause and a few measured sips from the glass that he was holding in his hand allowed him to go on stringing together threats and warnings. Standing at his side, his daughter spoke not a word; she appeared to be counting the floor tiles with her fingers hidden in the sleeves of her habit. She looked to be so firmly in command of the situation, so increased in stature in the shadow of her father, so sure of herself, that it was not even necessary for her to speak, to render an account of the most recent events, which she had no doubt explained to him by letter. She was content now merely to cast a glance at her rivals from time to time, allowing them to surmise what her father was leaving unsaid, leading them to understand that the fate of the house was in his hands.

"As for the election," the latter went on, "do not allow yourselves to waste any more time in idle discussions, for such is the human condition that we often forget its principal end, becoming absorbed in the most superficial and incidental details. It is a great shame to see this house without a head to govern it, when in the past total peace and perfection resided in it. You would do well to set aside doubts and concerns, for I shall lend you my aid and support the moment you elect a new superior."

As he spoke these words, his eyes strayed toward the one who, having asked his help, now appeared to be completely aloof from everything that was going on.

"And so, sisters, my daughters, I regard myself as being a good father to all of you. And therefore I advise all of you to be of good cheer and to forget all of your past factional quarrels."

The community remained as silent as a bunch of schoolboys after a stern lecture from their master, conceling only with the greatest difficulty their yearning to answer back, all of them of one mind and not moving a single step toward the door. And seeing them so firm in their resolve, our protector, reluctant to leave by himself and perhaps hoping that they would accompany him to the door, asked:

"Do any of Your Mercies take objection to anything that I have said?"

And his face immediately turned bright red as he listened to the reply.

"May the grace of the Holy Spirit be with Your Excellency. As regards the new prioress, this community prays you to understand that it would be a violation of its rules were we to proceed to hold such an election so long as the saint's trial has not been ended."

For a moment our protector stood there, his lips tight shut, deep in thought, as the same voice added:

"Furthermore, if our sister returns having been adjudged innocent, it would be a grave affront to her."

"Such an eventuality is not going to come about," he muttered in an irate tone of voice.

"How, milord, may we be certain of that?"

"I shall discuss the subject with the provincial, and he will send word as to what we decide."

With these words he abruptly ended the interchange, and more swiftly this time, with furrowed brow and a heavy tread, he left the room and the convent.

He spent all of the following day in the city. He was later seen twice alone with his daughter. Not one of the sisters in the house was again admitted to his presence, not one of them was allowed to plead with him, question him, or ask him to intercede with the Tribunal to bring such a long trial to as swift a conclusion as possible. Any and every attempt to do so was thwarted by a discreet wall in the form of an impassive secretary.

And yet his one concern, in the city as in the house, was the future of his daughter who, according to someone who managed to catch a glimpse of them walking together in the convent garden, was pressing him with heartfelt words and sighs, urging him to take up the reins of the trial in his own hands, telling him of her many trials and tribulations, and perhaps even threatening to leave the house if the situation was not resolved soon.

On the following night he left. Our guest went out to the portico to bid him goodbye. And as she bowed to kiss his hands, those of us around her overheard her final reminder:

"Remember, my esteemed father," she had said, "that if she returns there is no use in my remaining here."

And her father, his eyes taking in the entire house at one glance, again answered, his face set in a resolute expression:

"Set your mind at rest on that score. I will see to it that the situation is resolved as soon as I arrive at court."

It was still early in the morning and yet already the sun's warmth had set the earth to murmuring with the chirr of the cicadas, the song of the scorpions, half asleep in their nests of dust, the wind about to die away beneath the poplars, amid the tree trunks eaten away by flies and grubs. It was still early when the procession disappeared behind the hills, bright still with a thousand cloudy mirrors, green broom thickets, dry, split tree trunks which to our eyes, just barely able to make them out, were a harbinger of the fate that step by step was advancing toward us across the plain, slowly and pitilessly, ready to sweep us away with its cruel arm.

Chapter Eight

THAT beam of sunlight that every so often would fall upon my eyes, telling me that the door of my cell was opening, suddenly cast its bright light upon me at an unexpected hour. As always, it brought with it the keeper, who on this occasion had not come alone, but instead followed by two other persons whom I did not know but who, to judge from the pomp and circumstance surrounding them, I took to be familiars of the Holy Office.

They closed the cell door after them and after enjoining me repeatedly to keep secret everything that I had seen, heard, or suffered up until then, asked me whether I had been treated well thus far, in particular with regard to food and cleanliness, whether over such a long period of time I had suffered any sort of illness or diminution of my strength, and whether I found myself of sound mind and prepared to listen to everything they had to communicate to me.

I agreed that I had suffered no illness or ailment and was as sound in mind and body as the day I was confined to that cell, and as they searched about in their garments for the document on which my sentence was recorded, I tried my best to see their faces, which I could just barely make out in that dim shadow. But more than their faces, which I could not manage to see clearly, it was their grave and circumspect tone of voice, the solemn way in which the document was read to me by the light of the narrow little window that told me that they were highly placed officials.

That voice gave a detailed account, not only of our sin but of its sad and serious consequences. It explained how we had come to fabricate the false wounds, the miraculous stigmata, thereby doing grave harm to ourselves and to the house, giving rise to deception and scandal of which many other cities and persons were victims. The one thing in our favor was the fact that the Tribunal had found no signs of heresy, but rather mere trickery, the fruit of our ignorance in so special and dangerous a domain. Hence, in view of the time that we had already spent in prison, the Tribunal was inclined to show clemency. It condemned the saint to abjure, in the presence of her faithful followers, her many errors and leave the house, whereupon she would be obliged to seek another in which, as a simple guest in residence she was to be deprived for ten full years of an active vote in the chapter and merely speak and listen for another ten unless she were granted a pardon. Hence, she would again be cloistered, though she would be subjected to all sorts of cruel privations. She would not be allowed to hear holy mass, to confess, or receive communion without the permission of the hierarchy to whose jurisdiction she was to be handed over.

The Tribunal further ordered that an edict be published in all the churches, towns, and villages in which she was still an object of worship, whereby all portraits, crosses, and relics appertaining to her were prohibited, as well as any and every sort of devotion in her honor, on pain of major excommunication.

I for my part was let off more easily. I too was to abjure before the community and abandon the house, but the rest of my sentence consisted of hearing masses and fasting, and a brief half-year of exile.

The moment the familiars and the guard departed, leaving me alone once more in my friendly semidarkness, I fell on my knees and gave thanks to Our Lord God for the great mercy He had shown me. I felt tears well up in my eyes, for so long empty and dry, and trickle silently down my cheeks. I saw myself in the sun once more, in the light of that courtyard, till then filled only with the sound of footsteps, the calls of swifts, and the ringing of bells; I felt as strong and vigorous as I once had, eager to run to the arms of my sister, never forgotten, ever-present though ill and far away. What would she be like now? Would she still be as haughty and unbending as before, or would so much time in prison have finally undermined her courage? What would her arms, her wounds, her hands look like now? Would the spread of that poison have been arrested, or would that dark blue evil still be threatening to consume her? According to her judges, she was still alive at least, and according to my heart she was still the same as always, despite our long separation and exile from the world.

August came round again, with its usual storms that awakened terrible echoes in the courtyards. It brought nothing new, except that during his usual visits, my keeper, aware of my sentence, seemed more talkative now, trying to brighten those last days of mine in that cell.

"As I see it, sister, you can only thank God. The two of

you didn't come out badly after all this. Except for death sentences, the rest never get carried out. Not to the letter at least. There are those who serve their prison sentences in their own homes, in convents and hospitals, there are those who go out during the day and stroll about and enjoy life with their family and friends and then come back to be locked up each night. Otherwise where would this Tribunal ever find enough jails to hold all the people that it sentences every year? Not even those condemned to imprisonment for life do more than two or three years. Things are worse for men who are condemned than for women: floggings or the galleys, if not exile and confiscation of everything they own."

Once the food had been brought, the water poured, and the remains of the meal removed, his thin silhouette grew dimmer as he headed toward the two stairs at the door. My eyes tried to follow him, but everything was becoming more blurred with each passing day. In the beginning I had attributed it to the feeble light that was all that entered the cell, but then one day there came back to my mind the memory of other sisters who were already old after suffering their first slight illnesses, a warning of other more serious ones to come. Up until then, I had never given a thought to my years, to the time that had gone by since they came to take us away, but as I struggled to make out the keeper and later to see even so much as the skin of my poor hands, already old, I realized that neither his vague silhouette nor the walls that I could no longer see distinctly were the signs of the time that had passed, age, death; these things were, rather, within me, in my pupils grown weary from so much darkness, in my failing sight struggling to discern signs of life around me.

It was as I faced yet another autumn, wondering whether

the visit from the familiars had been a figment of my imagination or a dream, that the door was one day thrown wide open, leaving me blinded with light and at the same time filled with hope. The same voice that had informed me of my sentence ordered me to gather together immediately all the tings that I wanted to take with me, but what belongings did I have to take with me? I was like a newborn babe, with nothing to my name except for my habit and my worn-out, broken-down sandals.

I said a brief prayer to bid farewell to those sad walls that for so long a time had been my only world, and with a last goodbye to my keeper, I followed my two new guards across the cloister garth and through the other inside courtyards. Overhead the stars were bunched together in dense white clusters, some with a steady gleam, the others twinkling. Below them there was only the clanking of keys in the darkness, as we went up empty stairways and down winding passageways.

My heart matched the rhythm of its beating to the sound of our footsteps, there was no taste in my mouth, my arms felt weak and helpless, my lips dry. My whole life was being reborn in the night, in that blind darkness, as though once beyond the door of my prison time past had vanished, all the years, the trials and tribulations blotted out forever.

On that long walk before the break of dawn, I realized that once again my entire life lay in this new meeting with my sister. We finally halted before the door of a second cell. One of the two shadows remained with me, while the other one turned the key that he had thrust into the darkness and called the saint by her name.

What a cruel wait, what harsh sounds, what a devoted passion made my poor heart pound as I waited for my sister to appear. She too, as poor and forgotten as I had been during all the time that we had been separated, probably had very little to bring with her.

A third shadow came to break the silence there beneath the stars, informing my guard that the cart was ready and asking at what hour the journey was to begin.

"It would be best to leave now."

"Now?" the other said in a surprised tone of voice. "What's the hurry? We could at least wait until it gets light."

"The Tribunal so wishes, to keep the news from getting round. They do not want her devotees to interfere with the journey."

"I'll do as the Tribunal wishes," the carter agreed.

Meanwhile the door in front of us opened. Despite the dark shadows, on merely recognizing her silhouette, her step, a light one now as though she were gliding over the tiles, a long-forgotten fire was kindled in my body, a renewed vigor brought me into her arms, blotting out our keepers, and the uneven flagstones that ripped the thin, worn leather of my sandals.

How frail and emaciated she felt in my arms! All skin and bones, as though she had just returned from being put on the rack; silent and broken. We stood there together in silence, lending each other strength, love, as though instead of a reunion this was our last farewell. There in the shadow, beneath the faint light coming from overhead, paying no attention to the voices of the three men who were still busy planning the journey, my sister and I burst into tears and sobs, without pause save for an occasional brief silence in which we carefully scrutinized each other.

"Jesus be with Your Charity. How are you?"

My sister raised her eyes above her veil, gazing at me with the same look as always.

"I am of good cheer. I bless this day that has come at last to put an end to our many miseries."

I was about to answer when our two keepers hurried us on. We obeyed their orders for the last time and soon reached the courtyard where the cart was waiting. I climbed in first and then tried to help my sister in, but as I tried to take her by the arms, I noted there in the dark that she drew them away. The carter came over and rather unceremoniously grabbed her by the waist, lifted her up, and stood her on the wooden floorboards of the cart. Then, a few moments later, after bidding the others goodbye as they went to open the gate for us, he climbed into the cart in turn, prodding his mule which very soon took us outside the walls.

This time the journey turned out to be less decorous and the atmosphere less companionable, for we had to hear the man's continual shouts of abuse at his poor old gray mule. Nothing but a ragged canopy protected us from the sun that climbed upward in the sky like a burning-hot coal till noon, to fall at last behind the horizon, leaving it as red as though a great fire were sweeping over the fields. The summer was saying farewell amid flashes of lightning and dust whirls. One afternoon it rained on us and before we could find shelter we were soaked to the skin, making it necessary for us to find an inn where we could dry off our clothes and our bodies so as to ward off tertian fevers.

By the light of the oil-lamp, as we hung our ragged habits

up to dry, I could barely make out what was left of that body that I had so long loved and remembered. Her skin now sagged everywhere, her once-pert breasts hung down, withered and dry, her flesh, still criss-crossed with faint scars, barely covered her frail ribcage.

And yet it was not that flesh that was the most terrible part of that ruined body, but her arms, dark, gnarled vine shoots, scarcely disguised by the dirty bandages wrapped around them.

"How are your wounds?" I asked as she awkwardly covered herself with the blankets in the room.

"I won't say that they're as well as I'd like them to be, nor will I deny that they're healing so badly that they cause me terrible pain at times."

"Will you not have them treated?"

"I would rather leave them as they are, as punishment for my sins."

And yet, despite her words, I would not put my hand in the fire to wager that she had repented. There was a spark of irony in her dull voice. Hence I asked her:

"And what do you think we ought to do now?"

"Do what the Tribunal has ordered us to do."

"And after that?"

"After that, the Lord will provide. We are in His hands."

Again that voice, again that look that long ago I understood so well. That night as least, we slept on a mattress, not on straw or on floorboards. We rose very early the following morning, and after we had said our prayers as usual, we wanted to go hear mass since we had seen a church near the inn, but the carter informed us that he couldn't wait, so that, with just a bit of bread in our bellies, we went on our way, happy despite everything, knowing that we were nearing the end of our journey.

And it was in that wasteland, beneath that punishing sun that scorched the wild olive trees and the stubble, that I discovered for the first time that I could not see as well as I once had. Before, when it was difficult for me to recognize my keeper in the darkness of the jail, I had always thought that it was a passing thing, that once outside, my former good eyesight would return.

But it did not. In the beginning, what with the happiness of my return to life, I didn't remember how much difficulty I had had seeing, but now, during the long days in the cart journeying through treeless countryside bristling with furze, that vague fog that blurred my eyes grew denser and denser.

At times I was able to make out my sister only with the aid of my memory, which added what my eyes were unable to see. Seeing me rub my eyelids till the tears came, she asked:

"What's the matter with your eyes, sister?"

"Nothing that can't wait till we reach the house."

"Be careful not to lean out of the cart. This sun and the dust we're raising are murderous."

I was inwardly ashamed at her concern for an ailment as inconsequential as mine when she was suffering from one so much worse in her hands and arms, with never a complaint. She must have been in a great deal of pain, for at times she fell silent, bearing up under the jolting of the cart as best she could, trying so hard to hold on and keep from crying out that her temples broke out in beads of sweat.

What a different journey this one was! Bad food, with but a single stop at midday, barely quenching our thirst, brought back to the house more or less secretly. A sad lot ours, a grave lack of respect for the saint who between cities and towns had had more than a hundred parishes at her feet!

Enduring such punishment, without a cloud to give us a little shelter from the sun, traversing fields as scorched as though struck by lightning, we made our way along very slowly, crossing flats of cracked mud and dry riverbeds, awaiting the moment when we would knock at the door of the convent. I tried in vain to catch a glimpse of it in the blur of dark evening shadows, but it was my sister who finally raised her voice, with a sigh of relief:

"Thanks be unto the Lord; we're here."

Somehow, without the carter's helping hand, the two of us were already at the door, pulling on the cord, making the bell ring loudly in the entryway.

And it was our good friend the lay sister who was the first to appear at the turning-box:

"Who is it?"

"Ave Maria; two sisters returning to this house."

It seemed to me that for all her slow-wittedness she realized almost at once who we were, judging from her haste to open the door for us. The moment we crossed the threshold, heading for the cloister, we understood why. Besides punishing us, the Holy Office had ordered the other sisters sent to other houses. Most of them were already in their new convents. Only the lay sister had remained behind to receive us, since the judge had decreed that the two ringleaders were to abjure their errors publicly, in the main church of the town, before those very same faithful who had for so long honored them.

Hence the house was deserted, a sad empty shell, in no

way prepared to welcome us; its chapel and cells empty, its irrigation ditch dry, its courtyards without a sign of life.

September came, the month that drains the earth's blood in the vineyards. October arrived with its first cold spells, but no time was a good time for my sister to comply with the first part of her penitence. She was never ready or willing to present herself before her devoted followers who, once they learned that we had returned, appeared once again with the same faith, refusing to smash or burn their relics and crosses. Warnings or threats were of no avail. They merely begged to see the saint again from the other side of the grille, to touch her hands as before. But my sister's time on this earth gradually grew shorter, as the dark poison of her hands spread, aiming at her heart, moving up her feeble arms.

My lay sister's hour came round too, a happy hour for her, for at last, after so many misfortunes, she saw her desires for a better, more peaceful life fulfilled, at a moment when she was least expecting it.

For some time she had often absented herself from the house. I thought that it was her eagerness to serve us that had caused her to take off somewhere. But time passed without her letting us know when she planned to leave us for good.

"How long are you planning to stay on with us?" I finally asked her one day.

"I'm in no hurry to leave, sister," she answered. "As long

as the two of you are here, I'll stay with you. What difference does it make if I'm in one house or another? My pleasure in serving the two of you is better satisfied in this one than in some other place that the Tribunal might decide to send me. What's more, as you know, I haven't yet taken my formal vows."

"Be that as it may, it would be best to obey the Tribunal. Let's not see you take any steps to oppose its decisions."

"Why should I? It must have far too much to occupy its attention for it to remember this humble sinner."

She said no more, but her tone of voice seemed to hint at happy new developments that she was keeping to herself. And hence she continued to serve us most cheerfully or walked along the portico singing a gay little song that was a striking contrast to the gloomy, empty cells.

But her many attentions, along with my own, brought no improvement in the saint's health; her nights were still restless, her awakenings accompanied by deep moans. The disease sown by me, never arrested by the doctor, who even now occasionally visited her, spread implacably, gaining time on time, devouring minutes, hours of health as well as the shreds of that miserable flesh.

In the house, a ruined shell beneath the silent belfry, only the lay sister seemed to keep up her spirits, to remain in good form, what with her furtive departures and her voice bringing the garden paths overgrown with weeds to life. Finally, one morning at midday, I discovered the reason for the change in her: it was none other than that truck gardener who had taken us in his cart to my father's village.

At first I did not recognize him as he stood there at her side, but he immediately came over to greet me.

266

"What's this, sister? Don't you remember me?" And seeing that I still wasn't certain who he was, he went on: "Here I am, ready and willing as I was back then to take you wherever you need to go."

"May the Lord repay you for your solicitude."

"And what about the saint? How is her health?"

"Not too good."

"The Lord grant that she too may soon be up and about. When the day comes that they close the house, don't fail to send word to me. After all, I emptied almost the whole of it all by myself, what with the many trips I made with my cart. I've never traveled about as much as I have in these months since the Tribunal decided to break up the convent. Not that I question its decisions. I'm ignorant when it comes to such things, but having known it when it was so prosperous, it seems a pity to see it fallen on such sad days and in such a sorry state."

"It's of little use to bewail the fact."

"That's quite true, but it strikes me nonetheless that neither the provincial nor even the bishop was up to doing everything that the good name of the order deserved."

"They must have their reasons."

"The fact, perhaps, that there are those who, out of fear or self-interest, do not wish the saint's fame to become unduly exalted. There are even those who are of the opinion that other convents were jealous of your protector's promises, especially after his daughter announced her intention of taking her vows in this one. Mayhap they feared that they would be left with less property and fewer alms if he began to give more generously to this house. In any event," he added thoughtfully after a pause, "that's how things go in this world;

some out of fear, others out of petty interests, are one and all out to destroy the weakest ones, as meanwhile the powerful, what with their bulls and their sales taxes, prosper, year after year, boasting the while of how compassionate they are."

"But what do those who are above us have to fear?" I reasoned in turn.

"As regards purity of blood, nobody is above anybody else," the gardener replied. "From the highest to the lowest, everyone fears that some relative they hadn't thought of, a Moor or a Jew, will come to light and end up burning at the stake. With life as complicated as it is, who can guarantee that his grandparents were descended from old Christian families? That's why even Provincials do their best to avoid any sort of trial and try to keep their distance from the Holy Inquisition, just as my companion here hopes to do."

I looked at the lay sister and said in astonishment:

"Has she also had dealings with the Tribunal?"

"No, sister, but she doesn't want to obey its decisions. And there are others who were in this convent who think the same way she does."

"About what?"

"What do you suppose? They don't understand why righteous sisters should have to pay for ones who sin, why they should be driven out of this convent without even having been accused of any misdeeds. A number of them are thinking of appealing to Rome, and others of going back to their homes."

The gardener looked at the lay sister as though urging her to speak. I then learned from her own lips that like others she was thinking of leaving the path of the Lord.

"So you want to leave the order?"

"I'm thinking of putting the habit aside."

I was confused and surprised. Despite the long time that had passed, I still remembered her telling me of her fervent love for the house, for the life of the cloister, protected from the evils of the world that lay in wait outside.

"That was when the convent was united," she answered. "But not now when there is so much discord. You don't realize it, Your Charity, because you've been gone for such a long time, but in the last few months, there was no torment or madness that did not find fertile ground in it, abandoned as it was by the hand of God and at the mercy of the guest's whims."

"But she's no longer here. You won't be likely to meet her again, no matter where they take you."

"I don't want to run the risk. I'd a thousand times rather be a laywoman than go to another house full of women. I've come to detest them so much that even if I were on the verge of dying I couldn't stand to have them at my side."

For the very first time after so many months, I felt like laughing. My poor friend, my traveling companion, my sister, so ready and willing to follow men the moment they asked her, despite their affronts and slights. Where, I wondered, might her unscrupulous friar be now? Whom would he be taking in by his clever lies now if the Tribunals had not yet put an end to his misdeeds?

I did not want to remind her of him, seeing her so happy with her gardener, whose eyes returned her gaze with a love multiplied many times over. On the contrary, as though approving of her decision, I asked her:

"And where are you planning to live? Do you have money or land?"

"These two hands are the only thing I possess," she answered in a determined voice, holding them out to me.

"And these hands of mine that will not fail her," her companion added. And so it was that I learned that they were planning to marry. What with all his going and coming, transporting sisters in his cart, the gardener had grown fond of her, and even though he was a widower, with children already grown, the lay sister had said yes, and they had agreed to hold the wedding once the convent was empty.

I also found out the unfortunate end that had awaited our guest's gallant suitor; a stray musket bullet had left him crippled in both legs in that far-off war we kept hearing about.

A sad cortege his, as he arrived lying on a simple litter, whereupon he was granted only the most grudging reception from his lady, who could scarcely be persuaded to come downstairs from her cell. One would think that she was receiving some distant relative, some friend of her father's and not that submissive suitor who had come to visit her in days gone by.

Seeing him lying there before her doing his best to ease his pain, she had asked him:

"What about my father? Does he know?"

"It happened only a few steps away from where he was."

"Why didn't he send me word?"

"I begged him not to. In the beginning, I thought I would be well soon enough to arrive here before the news did." He pressed his lips tightly together and did his best to rise to his feet, but try as he might, his legs remained motionless. "A hard fate to bear, this," he murmured despite himself. "Being at once alive and dead, bound fast like Tantalus and yet as free as the day I was born. Has anyone ever suffered worse torment?"

"The Lord in His mercy will take pity on you."

"I'd prefer the services of a good surgeon. I know one at court who has put invalids worse off than I am back on their feet. Until such a time you will not have to put up with me again. May God be with you."

"May He restore you to health."

"If, as I hope, that man I have been speaking of repairs my bones, I'll be back very soon to get you."

The guest did not answer. She stood there looking at him as the soldiers lifted up that body overcome at once by passion and pain.

Seeing him carried off thus, a few inches above the ground, just barely above the mud, after having galloped up one day proudly seated on his steed, dashing and determined, brought tears to the eyes of some of the sisters, of all of them, most likely, except for the one who must have been most deeply moved by that unhappy departure.

Perhaps she remembered him for a short time but she soon began once again to spend her days eagerly waiting for the arrival of the courier, for news of the saint's trial, which already in those days was still dragging on and on. No one was surprised that she was no longer at all concerned about the young man who at that moment was perhaps fighting for his life. Closed up in her cell, protected from the world round about her by her long hours of waiting and her idle pursuits, nothing beyond its walls mattered to her except the triumph or the death of my sister and friend.

When the lay sister bade me goodbye, I remained in the

portico for a long time, meditating alone, asking myself what clay that miserable queen placed in the house by our protector as a seed of discord could be made of. I thought that at worst the Lord had already prepared His hell for us, decided what punishment should be ours, even before my sister and I planned the deed that would offend Him, even before we deceived the community. Such are His powers, and such also must be His secret designs.

Everything now depended on my sister's health, on her hands, as before her trial and even before that.

One afternoon, as I was on my knees in the chapel praying to God to restore her health, I heard a knock at the door at the entrance, and since the lay sister was not there, I went out to the turning-box despite the rain that was falling. The heavens had opened upon the cloister, and the rain that was pouring down was sweeping the plaster, the broken roof tiles toward the drains that had been stopped up for months now. The ground between what had once been flowering hedgerows had now turned into a dirty sea, over which waterbugs and spiders were navigating in all directions in great long strides. The doves had long since flown away, following after the sisters; the swifts were no doubt huddled up in their feathers in the joints of the rafters; all creatures, from the most humble to the least venturesome, seemed to be awaiting, in the shadows pierced by floods of light, the final destruction of the house, its total collapse beneath the weight of the water, of the contempt and the abandonment we had brought upon it by our sins, which had in no way been extirpated.

I myself no longer thought of it in the same way as I had in the days when, together with my sister, I explored at random the secret paths of the garden, when we would meet alone in its crossways and in its corners, in that pleasant meadow, in the shade of the poplars. Now nothing of that existed for my blind eyes, only the sound of rain, of violent, hostile torrents of water and the dull rumbling of the clouds that were a prelude to flashes of lightning.

Even the saint seemed only half alive these days, lying begridden, gotten up once a day by me, and merely waiting for the hour when she would present herself before the Lord rather than before the ever-dwindling flock of her faithful. Nowadays not even they pushed and shoved and knocked each other down on the broad esplanade outside. As though time or fear had made them less active because they were more wary, they now came knocking on the door only from time to time, like the ones at present, whose pounding on the door continued to echo as I tried to make my way toward them amid the wind and the rain. There the two of them were—two women—wetter than I was, waiting in the shelter of the arches.

"Ave Maria," I murmured through the turning-box. "What may I do for you at this hour?"

"We beg Your Charity's pardon; we have come to bring this for the saint."

I tried to make out through the peephole what manner of alms it was that they were bringing. It looked to me like one more offering like so many others, a little basket covered with a skimpy cloth.

"Very well, leave it in the turning-box. I will see to it that it is brought to her."

I was heading back for the cell when I heard the box turn again at my back. I looked, and there now appeared before me a very small wooden cross. I heard the woman's voice again, as clearly as before.

"Couldn't you touch her habit with this cross, sister?"

"That is forbidden. Didn't you know?"

"Even so. You would be doing us a great favor."

"She is not a saint any longer," I answered in a vehement tone of voice, thinking that that would frighten the woman off. But it did not. On the contrary, as though she had not even heard me, she hastened to explain:

"It's for a son of mine who is sick with tertian fevers."

"The Holy Tribunal has forbidden it. It's posted on the door. Didn't you see it?"

"We don't know how to read, sister. In any case, even if you won't grant me this favor, may heaven keep you."

"May the Lord be with you."

The turning-box fell silent and I continued on my way with the basket in my hand, pursued by thunder and lightning. The rain was coming down in torrents, in heavy curtains that echoed loudly as they swept over walls and rooftops. Once beneath the shelter of the arches with their frightening shadows, I soon left the cloister behind and entered the inside patio, near the other smaller one onto which the cells opened: all of them abandoned now, their doors ajar, white burrows whose interiors lay exposed. All that was left in them were a few straw mattresses half split apart, rotting from the dampness, filthy with mold, debris that had once been chairs, and here and there an abandoned holy image. It was as though a

274

band of demons had wallowed about inside them, destroying everything they found in their path, from the most humble objects to the most exalted.

Undoubtedly the sisters had left the house most happily, as the lay sister had assured me our guest had. The latter would most likely end up at court as she so eagerly desired, though before she did she might be obliged to pass through other convents, none as miserable as this one, from which she had not even troubled to take with her anything save her silver table service and jewels and some of her most costly furniture.

On the day of her departure, even though the familiars of the Holy Tribunal were waiting at the door, she had lingered in her cell, explaining that she was not prepared to travel at midday with the sun beating down overhead. Later on she had asked for yet more time so as to write to her father to protest against her removal to another house, and she had declared that it was necessary to wait until her courier arrived, since despite the fact that she had affixed her seal to the letter, she insisted that she must personally hand it over to him.

The familiars agreed to everything she asked, in view of her rank if not her office, since she was not to assume her functions as prioress until the community, once its sin had been expiated, was again reunited.

As the lay sister told it, late afternoon arrived and mistress and maidservant were still busy packing.

"What shall we do with your dresses, milady?" the girl asked.

"Pack as many as you can and leave the rest behind."

"Even this satin one? You might change your mind, milady; you might need it later. In all sincerity, may I say that rather than a nun, I see you more readily at court, where you will have no lack of gallant suitors."

"You may leave it behind nonetheless. There will be many others like it in my father's house."

"Do you mean to say, milady, that we are no longer going to take vows?"

"Hurry up there with your packing. Who knows?"

"Your wish is my desire. As far as I'm concerned, it doesn't matter either way, as long as I am at your side."

And so her cell remained vacant after her departure, as lifeless as it was now, a silent mirror of her vacillations.

And so I went on my way, heading toward my sister's cell with that basket that could still serve to assuage our hunger.

I reached her door, and murmuring an "Ave Maria. In what health do you find yourself?" as usual, I began to make my way to her bedside across the room in the dark. My first thought was that because of the cold she would have pulled the blankets up over her, but they were lying on the floor at the foot of the bed, as in summer when the heat is stifling. So my sister had left her cell then. Perhaps she was in the chapel. I was pleased at the thought, for it seemed like a sign that her strength was returning. But the chapel was as empty and as dark as ever. I went out into the patio and called in a low voice:

"Sister! Can Your Charity hear me?"

The rain had almost stopped and overhead, amid bright clouds, the moon was sailing through the sky.

"Sister!" I called again.

There was no answer. The last rush of water in the roof gutters, the murmurs of the secret channels of the irrigation ditch filled the cloister with vague sounds, none of which was the one that I was waiting to hear, my sister's soft, solemn voice.

I looked for her in the kitchen, in the empty larder, in the old stable that later on had been turned into a tool storeroom. I even went to look in the irrigation ditch, full to overflowing, like a lake of silver imitating the moon. I peered into its depths, but its troubled waters, as cloudy as my eyes, sent back no reply.

Returning now, weary of shouting, with only my hands to guide me in the dark, I found myself once more in the corridor lined with cells.

Little by little, trying to calm the pounding of my heart, imagining various eventualities, I took a lamp to light my way and looked inside each cell until I had inspected that of every sister in the entire community. And as I left the very last one, there came to me, like a wind clearing my head, the memory of the guest of the house.

And there my sister was, in her cell, sitting in front of the silver mirror, dressed in her satin robe, with her head toppled over onto her chest.

Strangely enough, the light in my hand did not tremble. It was as though I had known beforehand that she must be there, surrounded by all the things that her enemy had left for time to devour, the single heiress of a life that she must have desperately yearned for.

Her two motionless arms, the path whereby the Unforgiving One was to come to meet her, were hanging down pointing to the floor. Her bandages of clumsily darned rags had come loose, like filthy strips of bark, from the black, mortified tendons. Even so, despite the stench, despite her terrible eyes, wide-open, fixed in an empty stare, I took her in my arms, trying to raise her to her feet one more time, to catch the sound of her voice, to feel her wounded body next to mine. But this time she did not speak, or totter on her feet, or turn her pupils toward me; she merely began to slip out of my arms and fall toward the floor, not just dead but desiccated.

I dragged her as best I could, more or less feeling my way in the darkness, to the bed, and once I had laid her down on it, I fell to my knees, and began to pray for her, offering the Lord my life in exchange for hers, my badly damaged health in return for her recovery, my own salvation to redeem her from eternal damnation.

But who was I to judge her, who was I to know whether the Lord had taken her to Him in grace, or whether it was Satan who had dragged her down to hell with him? Who was I, filled with contrition and at the same time a rebel against the world and the community, against my own faith and the common destiny that had ended there alongside that battered corpse?

There she lay, distant and indifferent, dressed for a fiesta at court, sleeping, awaiting who knew what sound or music to lead the dance outside the mirrors of the cell. Beneath the voluminous shining skirt the cork-soled clogs, too small to fit properly, revealed weary feet grown flat and broad after years of heavy work. The olive-colored hands on which the map of veins traced the route of our shared deceit, could barely be joined together now because of the deep creases of the palms and the gnarled fingers. The lineaments of her body could only be guessed at, like the curve of her neck eaten away by the disease, and the hair grown thin and sparse after having been hidden for so long.

Here at my feet is my entire life—my senses, my pleasure, my pride, my companion and mother. Who can abandon her? Who can allow them to strip her naked and dress her in the patched, oft-mended habit that the sisters are traditionally buried in? It will be necessary to watch over her this night, to fight for her as I fought for her in life, to accompany her, to defend her. For it is my life that I am defending in her, my salvation that lies in her hands, my destiny and my reason for being that is born and dies in her, in that body victorious once upon a time and today the seed of nothing, empty and dead. Let no one touch my love, let no one approach our bed and our nest, let no one lay a hand on these hands, so gentle and courageous. Let no one come disturb her sleep, to bury her in that other bed of ashes and lime that will receive the narrow, clumsily carpentered coffin. Too small a hiding place for two; no one will take us to that corner where the cypresses flourish, where the fruit on the vines does not ripen and bear seed and serves only for food for crows and rooks. I do not want to feel my poor eyes become more useless still, blinded by broken stone and sand; I want to see the black hills beyond the walls that mark off this miserable plot of ground. No one is going to separate us. I shall wait for our common punishment to end. When, Lord, will our time of glory, so long promised, finally come? Here we are, the two

279

of us trusting in that love of Thine that is able to save us, to turn our misery into happiness, to show us that path that leads to Thee, like a joyous flame rising toward the clouds.

We shall follow this path together. No one can drag me away from her bed of esparto grass. It will be necessary to lift us up together, take us away together, bury us together.

Those cypresses with their tops lopped off will watch over our sleep, the miserable vine will cover us with its bitter fruits, and the October wind that sweeps everything away before it, will sweep our names away forever. No one else will disturb this last secret union. That corner of the cloister will be our final kingdom till the day when You call us.

The two of us, far from sisters and prioresses, will live forever, praying Thee that as long as the world endures, no one will come to awaken us, that no one will come to take us from this peaceful bed in which the two of us love in solitude and wait.